IELTS

FOR ACADEMIC PURPOSES: A SHORT INTENSIVE COURSE

Malcolm Mann & Steve Taylore-Knowles

BANDSCORE BOOSTER

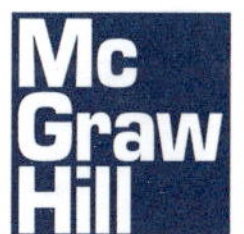

1 THE ARTS

Reading

Student's Book pages 18–19

Wordbank

Vocabulary from the Wordbank on page 19 of the Student's Book

A Write a verb in the correct form in each gap.

bring ~~emphasise~~ release

1 Some reggae music *emphasises* the problems of poverty.
2 They've recorded their new CD but they haven't ________ it yet.
3 They're planning to ________ out their next album to coincide with the start of their world tour.

B Write a word from the Wordbank in each gap. The first letter of each word is given to help you.

1 Most teenagers dream of being in a rock **b**________ at some point.
2 Would you describe this **s**________ of architecture as modernist or art deco?
3 With **a**________ art, it's pointless to ask the question: what is this a picture of?
4 The documentary **h**________ the problems of living in a big city.
5 With most modern cartoons, the **a**________ is all done on computer.

▸▸▸ Other vocabulary

Other vocabulary from the Reading section on pages 18 and 19 of the Student's Book

C Match to make phrases.

1 art	6 indie	A feature	F technology	1E	____
2 cave	7 number	B times	G album	____	____
3 debut	8 physical	C rock	H being	____	____
4 digital	9 prehistoric	D of art	I painting	____	____
5 human	10 work	E form	J one	____	____

D Write the correct form of the word in bold in each gap.

1 It's very difficult to date ancient art *accurately* (**ACCURATE**).
2 Ballet is a ________ (**SPECIFY**) type of dance.
3 Picasso's paintings are often immediately ________ (**IDENTIFY**) because of his unique style.
4 Full-length ________ (**ANIMATION**) children's films are very popular at the moment.
5 Opera is ________ (**TRADITION**) sung in Italian.
6 The concept of the 'chorus' ________ (**ORIGIN**) from ancient Greek drama.

Vocabulary boost: topic vocabulary

E Write the words for people formed from these words.

1	art	*artist*	**6**	paint	________
2	write	________	**7**	dance	________
3	song	________	**8**	poem	________
4	music	________	**9**	create	________
5	act	________	**10**	invent	________

F Complete the definitions with one of the following words.

audience **eyewitness** **listener** **onlooker** **spectator** ~~**viewer**~~

1. *viewer* : someone watching a TV programme
2. ________ : someone watching a sporting event in the place where it's happening
3. ________ : someone listening to the radio
4. ________ : someone who sees an accident or crime
5. ________ : someone who watches an event (such as a rescue) but doesn't take part
6. a member of the ________ : someone watching a live artistic performance in the place where it's happening

G The words in italics are in the wrong sentence. Find the correct words and write them on the lines.

1. We're going to get a local artist to paint a/an *instrument* of my grandmother. *portrait*
2. There's an interesting *portrait* on tonight about space travel. ________
3. Her very first role was in a school *performer* when she was eleven years old. ________
4. A *novel* in a musical has to be able to sing and dance as well as act. ________
5. Tolstoy's *play* 'War and Peace' is over 1,300 pages long! ________
6. Every child should learn to play a musical *documentary*, in my opinion. ________

Vocabulary boost: phrasal verbs

H Choose the correct word.

1. I'm thinking of checking **in** / **out** that new record shop tomorrow.
2. Would the Arctic Monkeys have caught **on** / **off** so quickly without MySpace?
3. I'm thinking of setting **out** / **up** a local drama club.
4. I generally just hang **over** / **out** with my friends at the weekend.
5. I gather they've done **down** / **up** the old police station and turned it into a museum.
6. I can't make **out** / **up** what this is supposed to be a picture of.

Student's Book page 20

Listening

Wordbank

Vocabulary from the Wordbank on page 20 of the Student's Book

A Choose the correct word to complete the gaps in this text.

1	**A** present	**B** contemporary	**C** actual
2	**A** exhibition	**B** revelation	**C** vision
3	**A** gallery	**B** monitor	**C** showcase
4	**A** phrasebook	**B** manual	**C** catalogue
5	**A** drawings	**B** sculptures	**C** paintings

NEW DIRECTIONS

Those of you who are interested in (**1**) ______ art should make a note of the dates of *New Directions*, a collection of paintings and photographs from some of the art world's most promising young artists. From July 1st to August 12th, this (**2**) ______ offers a rare opportunity to see challenging works from tomorrow's stars. Held at the A1 Studio, a large private (**3**) ______ , it promises to surprise, delight and shock. According to the (**4**) ______ , which lists over two hundred works, 'this could be the biggest thing in art for over one hundred years'. Okay, it's a pretty big claim, but there are some exciting artists here and works range from computer-generated images to good old-fashioned oil (**5**) ______. Contact A1 Studio to book a place.

▸▸▸ *Other vocabulary*

Other vocabulary from the Listening section on page 20 of the Student's Book

B Complete the table. Include negative forms.

Verb	Noun(s)	Adjective(s)	Adverb(s)
colour	colour	(1) ______ (2) ______ coloured colouring	(3) ______
confuse	(4) ______	(5) ______ (6) ______	(7) ______
criticise	(8) ______ (9) ______	(10) ______ (11) ______	(12) ______
dramatise	drama (13) ______	(14) ______	(15) ______
–	emotion	(16) ______ (17) ______ emotionless emotive	(18) ______ (19) ______
forget	–	(20) ______ forgettable unforgettable	unforgettably

Vocabulary boost: periods of time

C **Read the sentences, then on the line provided, write the word that matches the definition.**

A The rainy **season** in Japan runs from the beginning of June to the middle of July.
B I'm on holiday for the next **fortnight**, but we can meet when I get back.
C The results for the last **quarter** show that sales have increased.
D I think the 70s was a great **decade** for art and design.
E Picasso was probably the most famous artist of the 20th **century**.
F Many countries held celebrations in 2000 to mark the start of a new **millennium**.

1 two weeks: *fortnight*
2 1,000 years: ____________
3 ten years: ____________
4 three months (used in financial contexts): ____________
5 100 years: ____________
6 part of the year with different weather: ____________

Vocabulary boost: word formation

D **The words below all form verbs using *-ise*. Fill in the gaps with the correct forms of the words.**

advert economy familiar fantasy ~~final~~ modern personal sympathy

1 Let me know when you *finalise* your plans for this weekend.
2 I always ____________ my schoolbooks by sticking photos I like on them.
3 I ____________ with your problem, and I wish there was something I could do to help.
4 If you want people to know about your exhibition, you need to ____________ it in the local paper.
5 Make sure you ____________ yourself with the instructions before you start painting.
6 I've always ____________ about becoming a world famous artist.
7 We're ____________ now that I've lost my job so we can't afford a holiday.
8 They're ____________ the city centre because everything is starting to look quite old.

Vocabulary boost: topic vocabulary

E **CD, 1 Listen and write in each gap the correct word to match the definition.**

1 *fine* art: paintings, etc., that are beautiful and interesting
2 ____________ art: a type of art where the artist acts, dances, paints, etc., in front of an audience
3 ____________ art: a type of art where the main idea, often surprising or shocking, is more important than the work of art itself
4 ____________ art: a type of art that uses images and styles from advertisements, comic books, etc.

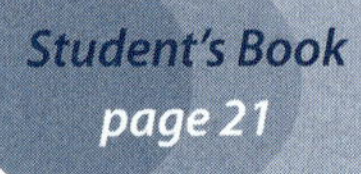

Speaking

Grammarbank: Talking about the present

Grammar Reference, Section 1, page 98 of the Student's Book

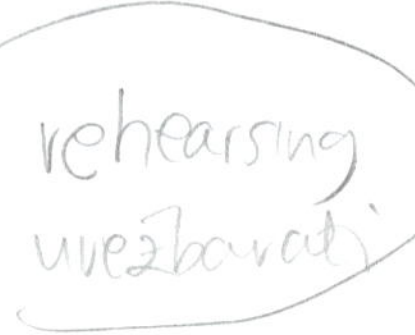

A **Choose the correct verb form.**

1 **I watch** / **I'm watching** this show every week without fail.
2 **I don't often get** / **I'm not often getting** the chance to go to concerts.
3 **We rehearse** / **We're rehearsing** right now so can I call you later on?
4 **Are you studying** / **Do you study** for your art history exam at the moment?
5 No, actually the CD **does have** / **is having** all the lyrics printed in the booklet.
6 **Do you know** / **Are you knowing** how to play any instruments other than the piano?

B **Use the correct form of the verb in brackets to fill in the gaps. Use contractions (I've, etc.) where possible.**

1 *I haven't drawn* (**I / NOT / DRAW**) a picture since I was at school!
2 ________________ (**YOU / ALREADY / HEAR**) the new Radiohead album?
3 ________________ (**THE BOOK / SELL**) over a million copies so far!
4 It's the first time ________________ (**I / EVER / SEE**) them play live.
5 How many times ________________ (**SHE / DO**) a world tour?
6 ________________ (**LEE / WORRY**) all week about the performance tonight.
7 ________________ (**YOU / EVER / GO**) to a movie premiere?
8 ________________ (**I / TRY**) to finish this poem all morning but it's taking longer than I expected.

C **Write a word from below in each gap.**

already before ever for just since still ~~yet~~

1 They haven't announced how much the concert tickets are *yet*.
2 I've been writing short stories ________ I was about eight years old.
3 I haven't read the book yet – I've only ________ bought it!
4 We ________ haven't been to the Edvard Munch exhibition and it closes next week.
5 Have you ________ entered a screenplay competition?
6 I've never heard of Broken Social Scene ________. Are they a new band?
7 Have you finished decorating the cake ________? That was fast!
8 The programme's only been on ________ about five minutes.

D **CD, 2 Listen to this IELTS candidate answering questions in Part 1 of the Speaking Module. Decide whether the statements are TRUE or FALSE.**

1 She has been playing the piano for 3 years. **TRUE / FALSE**
2 She has been playing the guitar since she was 7 years old. **TRUE / FALSE**
3 She has been playing the trumpet for a long time. **TRUE / FALSE**
4 She has just finished reading *War and Peace*. **TRUE / FALSE**
5 She hasn't decided yet what to read next. **TRUE / FALSE**

Wordbank

Vocabulary from the Wordbank on page 21 of the Student's Book

E **Write one word in each gap.**

1 When did you decide to take *up* pottery as a hobby?
2 I never seem to have time ______ anything other than studying.
3 I'm not very keen ______ game shows, to be honest.
4 My parents are very keen ______ me to go to university.
5 Jamie doesn't have enough time so I've taken ______ as director from him.

F **Write 'many', 'a few' or 'lots' in each gap.**

1 There were *lots* of people there I knew.
2 How ______ people went to the concert?
3 They'd already sold quite ______ of the paintings.
4 There were so ______ CD players, I didn't know which one to get.
5 Only ______ actors become famous and successful.
6 I don't know how much art she produced in her lifetime but it was ______!

G **Choose the correct word.**

1 The tickets were really expensive **because** / **so** / **such** we decided not to get them.
2 The tickets were really expensive **because** / **and** / **but** we decided to go anyway.
3 The tickets were really expensive **because** / **so** / **and** they're one of the biggest bands in the world.
4 The tickets were really expensive but for concerts **such** / **so** / **and** as this they usually are.

Vocabulary boost: word patterns

H **Use the correct form of the verbs in brackets and add any necessary words to complete the sentences.**

1 I'm not very keen *on reading* (**READ**) poetry, to be honest.
2 Are you interested ______ (**HAVE**) ballet lessons?
3 I used to be able ______ (**DRAW**) really well but I'm out of practice now.
4 Do you think everyone's capable ______ (**LEARN**) a musical instrument?
5 I haven't managed ______ (**SELL**) my novel yet but I'll keep trying.
6 I really hope you succeed ______ (**GET**) your novel published.
7 My sister's about ______ (**GO**) to art school in Seoul.
8 I'm not very good ______ (**REMEMBER**) lyrics to songs.

Writing

Student's Book pages 22–23

Grammarbank: Using the passive

Grammar Reference, Section 2, page 99 of the Student's Book

A **Underline five mistakes in the passive voice in this text. Rewrite each verb form correctly in the space below.**

From the data which has presented in this table, it can see that the cinema is becoming less popular with young people aged 14–18. Although the cinema was mention as a leisure activity by 68% of 14- to 18-year-olds ten years ago, today the figure is only 59%. In contrast, 70% of 19- to 23-year-olds who questioned said that they go to the cinema at least twice a month. In the next age group (24- to 37-year olds), the cinema was been chosen by 65% of those asked.

1 *is presented* 3 ________ 5 ________
2 ________ 4 ________

B **Rewrite each sentence using an appropriate passive form.**

1 You can see a large increase over ten years.
A large increase can be seen over ten years.
2 They asked over a 1,000 people for their opinions.
____
3 Someone designed the study to discover attitudes towards forms of entertainment.
____
4 Almost half of the people surveyed described concerts as 'very enjoyable'.
____
5 They can solve this problem by encouraging more art education.
____

C **Complete the text by putting the verbs provided into their passive forms.**

The data which (**1**) *is provided/has been provided* (**PROVIDE**) in the table shows that modern art (**2**) ________ (**CONSIDER**) by many people to be shocking. Over 75% of the people who (**3**) ________ (**ASK**) to take part in the survey said that they (**4**) ________ (**SHOCK**) by a piece of modern art in the past. At the same time, modern art (**5**) ________ (**DESCRIBE**) as 'important' by over half of the people surveyed (53%). Traditional art (**6**) ________ (**PREFER**) by those over 50, with 85% saying that more exhibitions should (**7**) ________ (**ORGANISE**) by local museums. The percentage of over-50s who believed that young people would (**8**) ________ (**ATTRACT**) to such exhibitions was high at 79%. However, when young people themselves (**9**) ________ (**INTERVIEW**) as part of the survey, only 38% thought that youngsters could (**10**) ________ (**INTEREST**) in traditional art by such means.

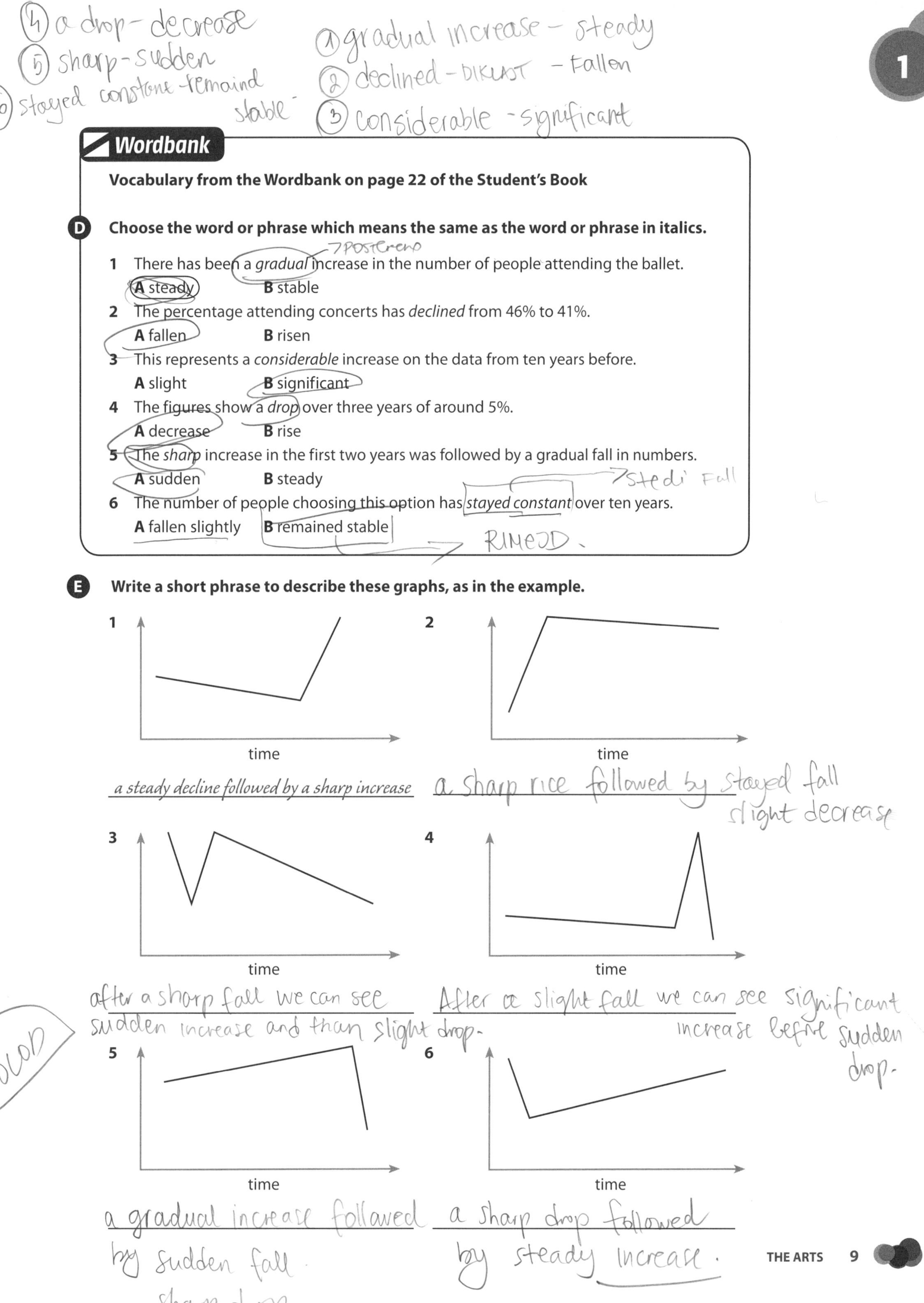

Wordbank

Vocabulary from the Wordbank on page 22 of the Student's Book

D Choose the word or phrase which means the same as the word or phrase in italics.

1 There has been a *gradual* increase in the number of people attending the ballet.
A steady **B** stable

2 The percentage attending concerts has *declined* from 46% to 41%.
A fallen **B** risen

3 This represents a *considerable* increase on the data from ten years before.
A slight **B** significant

4 The figures show a *drop* over three years of around 5%.
A decrease **B** rise

5 The *sharp* increase in the first two years was followed by a gradual fall in numbers.
A sudden **B** steady

6 The number of people choosing this option has *stayed constant* over ten years.
A fallen slightly **B** remained stable

E Write a short phrase to describe these graphs, as in the example.

1 time

a steady decline followed by a sharp increase

2 time

3 time

4 time

5 time

6 time

F **Look at this table and choose the correct word or phrase.**

Visits to the cinema	10 years ago (%)	today (%)
less than once per month	40	27
once per month	25	22
one to three times per month	20	23
more than three times per month	15	28

1 The number of people visiting the cinema less than once per month has dropped **significantly** / **slightly**.
2 There has been **a considerable** / **a slight** fall in the number visiting the cinema once per month.
3 The number of people who go to the cinema from one to three times per month has risen **considerably** / **slightly**.
4 The data show a **slight** / **considerable** increase over ten years in the number visiting the cinema more than three times per month.

Vocabulary boost: topic vocabulary

G **Match each type of picture to the correct description.**

1 cartoon ____	3 illustration ____	5 sketch ____
2 diagram ____	4 portrait ____	6 symbol ____

A This is a small picture that presents information, such as a warning, clearly and simply. You might see one of these in a guidebook.
B This is a painting or a photograph of a person. You might see this in a biography of that person.
C This is a drawing which is funny or which makes a political point. You might see one of these in a newspaper.
D This is a quick drawing, usually with a pencil. You might see this in somebody's notebook.
E This is a picture which goes with text and shows you what something being described looks like. You might see one of these in a children's storybook.
F This is a picture which shows you how a device or a process works. You might see one of these in an instruction manual.

Vocabulary boost: prepositions

H **Choose the correct word.**

1 Let me take a photo **of** / **from** you standing over here.
2 I think the statue is made **with** / **of** gold, isn't it?
3 The artist has used a special kind of paint which is made **of** / **from** plants.
4 I've never heard that piece of music played **on** / **by** the guitar before.
5 Da Vinci's famous painting, the *Mona Lisa*, hangs **at** / **in** the Louvre.
6 The artist has put a lot of emotion **into** / **onto** the painting.

1

EXAM PRACTICE

Student's Book pages 24–25

Reading

Vocabulary from the Reading text on pages 24 and 25 of the Student's Book

A **Find words or phrases in the Reading text which have a similar meaning to those below.**

1 changed version (paragraph 1) *adaptation*
2 examining, investigating (paragraph 1) ________
3 things, features (paragraph 1) ________
4 age, period of time (paragraph 2) ________
5 many (paragraph 2) ________
6 before (paragraph 2) ________
7 pictures (paragraph 2) ________
8 not having (paragraph 2) ________
9 realness, genuineness (paragraph 3) ________
10 said but not proved (paragraph 3) ________

B **These adverbs appear in the Reading text. Choose the best meaning for each one.**

1 primarily (paragraph 2) **at first / mainly**
2 nearly (paragraph 3) **a little more or less than / a little less than**
3 originally (paragraph 4) **at first / from the start until now**
4 highly (paragraph 4) **often / extremely**
5 partially (paragraph 5) **completely / not completely**
6 virtually (paragraph 6) **really / almost**
7 largely (paragraph 6) **mainly / having a big effect on**

C **Find a word from the Reading text to fill each gap.**

1 A large number of words are *common* to both English and French. (paragraph 1)
2 If you invent something, you should take out a ________ to stop other people making money from it. (paragraph 4)
3 If you ________ a business, you start it with someone else. (paragraph 4)
4 Which ________ of washing powder do you usually buy? (paragraph 4)
5 Most car manufacturers produce a number of different ________. (paragraph 5)
6 If you make your ________ on something, you have an effect on it. (paragraph 6)
7 If something's ________, you can't see it at all. (paragraph 6)
8 Her ________ collection of magazines was destroyed in the fire. (paragraph 6)

D **Find forms of these words in the Reading text.**

1 combine: *combination* (noun) (paragraph 1)
2 popular: ________ (noun) (paragraph 2)
3 exist: ________ (noun) (paragraph 2)
4 certain: ________ (noun, negative) (paragraph 3)
5 perform: ________ (noun) (paragraph 4)
6 major: ________ (noun) (paragraph 5)
7 develop: ________ (noun) (paragraph 6)
8 contribute: ________ (noun) (paragraph 6)

2 SOCIETIES

Reading

Student's Book pages 28–29

Wordbank

Vocabulary from the Wordbank on page 29 of the Student's Book

A Match to make phrases. If more than one phrase is possible, write all the possibilities.

1	welfare	A	benefit	1A, E, F
2	national	B	countries	______
3	developing	C	care	______
4	unemployment	D	insurance	______
5	health	E	rights	______
6	human	F	system	______

B Write a phrase from Exercise A in each gap.

1 The welfare system provides help for everyone at difficult times in their lives.
2 Some cities in developing countries are growing very quickly.
3 After finishing university, I lived on unemployment benefit for a year before I found a job.
4 People in Britain pay about 10% of their income on national insurance.
5 I believe there are basic human rights, like the freedom to practise one's religion.
6 I believe we should make health care free for everyone.

Other vocabulary

Other vocabulary from the Reading section on pages 28 and 29 of the Student's Book

C Choose the correct word.

1 I give money each month to three different **companies** / **charities**.
2 The country doesn't have the **fees** / **funds** to improve the road system.
3 The local **authorities** / **superiors** haven't done what they promised to do.
4 After the disaster, **shipments** / **sets** of food started to arrive.
5 The **roots** / **basics** of the problem lie in people's attitudes.
6 All **humans** / **citizens** of Europe are allowed to vote in these elections.

D Write a word from below in each gap.

aid co-operation ~~famine~~ ideal poverty trade

1 Millions of people died in the recent famine in the country.
2 Do you think we should increase the amount of aid we give to other countries?
3 World peace is a wonderful ideal, but is it really possible?
4 More should be done about the illegal trade in weapons.
5 Since the economy collapsed, a lot of people have been living in poverty.
6 It's going to take co-operation between different governments to solve the problem.

Vocabulary boost: word formation

E **Write the correct form of the word in bold in each gap.**

POLITICS

1 Many people don't trust *politicians*, but I think they are generally honest.
2 The country has faced a number of ____________ problems recently.
3 He was very ____________ active when he was younger.

ORGANISE

1 The ____________ of the protest claimed that 50,000 people were involved.
2 The government is so ____________ that nobody believes it will win the next election.
3 This problem can only be solved by a large ____________, like the United Nations.

LEGAL

1 I don't think they should ____________ handguns in this country.
2 I'm sorry. I didn't know it was ____________ to park here.
3 All passengers are ____________ required to complete the immigration form.

ECONOMY

1 The ____________ situation seems to be getting worse everywhere.
2 ____________ are predicting that things will get worse before they get better.
3 We need to find more ____________ ways of producing energy.

SOCIETY

1 It's not easy to solve ____________ problems, like poverty.
2 There's a big problem with ____________ behaviour and minor crime in this area.
3 In some countries, it's ____________ acceptable to ask someone how much they earn.

Vocabulary boost: phrasal verbs

F **Write a word from below in the correct form in each gap.**

bring come do get join ~~stand~~ turn vote

1 I'm quite shy and I don't like to *stand* out in a group of people.
2 My brother and I didn't really ____________ on when we were kids.
3 They're planning to ____________ in a new law that will make it illegal.
4 I think people are going to ____________ this government out.
5 They were discussing politics and I decided to ____________ in with them.
6 Things didn't ____________ out the way people expected.
7 When the new law ____________ in, things will get a lot better.
8 They should ____________ away with the National Health Service in my opinion.

Student's Book page 30

Listening

Wordbank

Vocabulary from the Wordbank on page 30 of the Student's Book

A **Write a word from the Wordbank in each gap. The first letter of each word is given to help you.**

1 You should learn about the habits and **c**ustoms ____________ of a place before you visit.
2 I wish I hadn't **v**________________ to help at the Student Welfare Service.
3 The university **c**________________ for the needs of students very well.
4 The biggest **i**________________ the plan faces is a lack of money.
5 I couldn't believe how **r**________________ Amy was to the governor.
6 I didn't really **f**________________ in when I went to university.

Other vocabulary

Other vocabulary from the Listening section on page 30 of the Student's Book

B **Choose the correct answer.**

1 There has been a big increase in the number of __A__ students.
A overseas **B** outside **C** abroad
2 Many people are ______ of the problem of culture shock.
A unfamiliar **B** ignorant **C** uneducated
3 I found it hard to ______ to life in another country.
A change **B** adjust **C** alter
4 Where is the event going to be ______ ?
A placed **B** held **C** happened
5 I was ______ satisfied with how my exams went.
A largely **B** finely **C** exactly
6 It's important to get help when you ______ problems so far from home.
A reach **B** greet **C** face

Vocabulary boost: topic vocabulary

C **Match each word to the correct definition.**

1	circle	**A**	a group of people who cause trouble or commit crimes	1F
2	club	**B**	a group of families who live together, usually in remote areas	______
3	gang	**C**	an organisation for people with similar interests	______
4	society	**D**	people in a country considered together and in general	______
5	tribe	**E**	a large group of people in the same place	______
6	crowd	**F**	a group of people who know each other as friends	______

D Choose the correct word.

1 I'm used to having quite a large social **circle** / **club** around me.
2 I've been reading about a **gang** / **tribe** in Brazil that has just been discovered.
3 I lost sight of my sister in the **society** / **crowd**.
4 We need to work together as a **society** / **circle** to solve the country's problems.
5 People are very concerned about **gangs** / **circles** of young people.
6 Why don't you think about joining a fishing **crowd** / **club**?

Vocabulary boost: phrases

E Write a verb from below in each gap. You need to use some verbs more than once.

do get make show take

1 ___*take*___ pity on someone
2 __________ someone a promise
3 __________ friends with someone
4 __________ your approval of something
5 __________ care of something/someone
6 __________ someone a favour
7 __________ something into account
8 __________ into debt

F Write the correct form of a phrase from Exercise E in each gap.

1 Everyone ___*showed their approval of*___ the decision by applauding loudly.
2 Could you ____________________ me ____________________ and tell Ping I won't be at the party?
3 It can be hard to ____________________ people when you first arrive in a foreign country.
4 The government has a responsibility to ____________________ the poor.
5 The plan doesn't ____________________ the economy ____________________.
6 It's very easy for students to ____________________ when they are at university.
7 Abdul ____________________ his wife ____________________ that he would give up politics.
8 I ____________________ the old man and gave him some money.

Student's Book page 31

Speaking

Grammarbank: Talking about the past

Grammar Reference, Section 3, pages 99–100 of the Student's Book

A **Each verb in bold is in the wrong tense. Write the correct tense on the line.**

1 We **were moving** to this area in 2007. *moved*
2 Before that, we **are living** abroad for a few years. were livins
3 When we **had lived** abroad, I knew lots of people. lived
4 When we first moved here, it **had been** difficult to meet people. was
5 After a while, though, I **was meeting** some people the same age as me. met
6 By the time we **lived** here for a year, I had lots of friends. had lived
7 Then I **had been starting** to go to a different school. started
8 I **had been missing** some of my friends, but I still saw them at the weekend. missed.

B **Rewrite each sentence using the phrase given. Make as many sentences as you can each time.**

1 I started work and the phone rang.
was working
When the phone rang, I was working. / I was working when the phone rang.

2 Tim left the party and then I arrived.
had left
____

3 I started my homework and you rang me ten minutes later.
had been doing
____

4 My parents moved abroad six months before I was born.
had been living
____

5 Wendy and Miguel knew each other for a year and then I met them.
had known
____

6 Liza and I started talking about Dan and then he came into the room.
were talking
____

7 Kyle finally arrived half an hour after I did.
had been waiting
____

8 We moved to France and I went to university while we were there.
were living
____

Wordbank

Vocabulary from the Wordbank on page 31 of the Student's Book

C **Write one word in each gap.**

1 It ___seems___ to me that people don't care about each other enough.
2 In my ___________, we all have a responsibility to help the poor.
3 From my ___point___ of view, the government needs to do something about the problem.
4 I tend to ___________ that society judges people too easily.
5 My ___________ opinion is that we pay too much in tax at the moment.
6 As ___________ as I'm concerned, it's time we made smoking illegal.

D **CD, 3 Listen to these people talking about a new law. Decide whether each speaker agrees or disagrees with the law.**

1 Speaker 1 (agrees) / disagrees
2 Speaker 2 agrees / disagrees
3 Speaker 3 agrees / disagrees
4 Speaker 4 agrees / disagrees
5 Speaker 5 agrees / disagrees
6 Speaker 6 agrees / disagrees

Other vocabulary

Other vocabulary from the Speaking section on page 31 of the Student's Book

E **Complete the table. Include negative forms.**

Verb	Adjective	Noun
excite	(1) ___exciting___ (3) ___________ (4) ___________	(2) ___________
–	(5) ___________	leaf
reside	(6) ___________	(7) ___________ (8) ___________

Vocabulary boost: places to live

F **Match each word or phrase to the correct definition.**

1 bungalow
2 detached house
3 mansion
4 semi-detached house
5 terraced house
6 villa

A a house that is separate from the other houses around it ___1C___
B a large house with a garden in a warm country ______
C a house with all the rooms on one level ______
D a house that shares walls with other houses on two sides ______
E a very large, luxurious house ______
F a house that shares a wall with one other house ______

Student's Book pages 32–33

Writing

Grammarbank: Conceding and contrasting

Grammar Reference, Section 4, page 100 of the Student's Book

A Write one word in each gap.

1 Some people commit crimes in spite *of* having spent time in prison.
2 He was sent to prison ______ his claims that he was innocent.
3 Despite the ______ that a witness identified her, she was found not guilty.
4 Crime is still increasing, ______ though there are more and more police.
5 ______ there was little evidence, he was still found guilty.

B Choose the correct answer.

1 We were robbed, despite *B* a really good alarm system.
A we have **B** having **C** of having
2 Nobody was arrested, even though ______ witnesses.
A being **B** there were **C** there being
3 In spite of ______ , he refused to accept that he was guilty.
A the evidence **B** being evidence **C** there was evidence
4 Although ______ the door, someone managed to break in.
A locking **B** having locked **C** I locked
5 He decided to steal the car, even though ______ it was illegal.
A he knew **B** knowing **C** of knowing
6 In spite of the fact ______ sent to prison, he didn't learn his lesson.
A of being **B** being **C** that he was

C Rewrite each pair of sentences as one sentence using the word given.

1 The gang made very careful plans. They were still arrested.
The gang *were still arrested, despite making very careful plans* (**DESPITE**).
2 Karl was under eighteen. They still sent him to prison.
They ______ (**THOUGH**).
3 He wore a disguise. The police still caught him.
In ______ (**FACT**).
4 Jane had lots of money. She still stole a mobile phone.
Jane ______ (**SPITE**).
5 I locked the car. It was still stolen.
The car ______ (**ALTHOUGH**).
6 Crime is dropping in this area. It's still a major problem.
Crime ______ (**EVEN**).

Wordbank

Vocabulary from the Wordbank on page 32 of the Student's Book

D Write one word in each gap.

1 From what he said, I *formed* the impression that he was guilty.
2 Crime seems to be falling, but most people ________ the belief that it's on the increase.
3 The police ________ the conclusion that the crime was committed by an employee.
4 The government ________ the view that the law needs to be changed.
5 I've gradually ________ to the conclusion that prison doesn't work.

▸▸▸ *Other vocabulary*

Other vocabulary from the Writing section on pages 32 and 33 of the Student's Book

E Rearrange the letters to make a word that fits in the gap.

1 What this problem needs is a new *approach* (**CAPAPROH**) based on scientific research.
2 Many in the local ________ (**MCNOYITMU**) are angry at the failure to prevent crime.
3 At this prison, we try to help the ________ (**FEFSNODRE**) understand how victims feel.
4 He was sentenced to 100 hours of community ________ (**VSEERIC**).
5 You can't blame the ________ (**CMIRCASESTCNU**) you grew up in for your behaviour.
6 The prison is home to approximately 500 ________ (**IASNTEM**).
7 The government hasn't done enough to ________ (**ACKETL**) crime.
8 The woman was ________ (**NVDCTEICO**) after a trial that lasted for three months.

F Match each word to the correct definition.

1	decent	A	not very large	____
2	ineffective	B	fairly good, not bad	____
3	limited	C	not willing to do something	____
4	minor	D	not very serious, unimportant	____
5	reluctant	E	not producing the desired results	____

G Choose the word from Exercise F which goes with each group of words.

1 *limited*
- results - resources - vocabulary - power

2 ________
- job - meal - wage - clothes - education

3 ________
- injury - crime - illness

4 ________
- solution - protection - attempt

Vocabulary boost: crimes and criminals

H **Write a word from below in each gap.**

arson blackmail burglary ~~forgery~~ fraud kidnapping
murder robbery theft vandalism

If someone is guilty of …

1 *forgery*, they create a fake version of something, such as a passport.
2 fraud, they get money by tricking people.
3 blackmail., they threaten to reveal a secret unless someone pays them money.
4 vandalism, they damage someone else's property.
5 robbery, they take money from someone, often with violence.
6 burglary, they take something from a building, such as someone's home.
7 kidnapping, they take someone and keep them until they receive some money.
8 murder, they kill someone.
9 theft, they steal something.
10 arson, they deliberately start a fire.

I **Write the word for the person who commits each of these crimes.**

1 arson *arsonist*
2 blackmail ____________
3 burglary ____________
4 forgery ____________
5 fraud ____________
6 kidnapping ____________
7 murder ____________
8 vandalism ____________
9 robbery ____________
10 theft thief

Vocabulary boost: word patterns

J **Write one word in each gap.**

1 find evidence *of* a crime
2 suspect someone of a crime
3 accuse someone of a crime
4 arrest someone for a crime
5 charge someone with a crime
6 try someone for a crime
7 find someone guilty/innocent of a crime
8 sentence someone to time in prison

K **CD, 4 Listen to this woman talking about a crime and decide whether the statements are TRUE or FALSE.**

1 The crime took place in her street. TRUE / (FALSE)
2 She was arrested for the crime. TRUE / FALSE
3 She was found guilty of the crime. TRUE / FALSE

2

EXAM PRACTICE

Student's Book pages 34–35

Reading

Vocabulary from the Reading text on pages 34 and 35 of the Student's Book

A Write a word from below in the correct form in each gap.

~~ancestor~~ diner individual

1 Your *ancestors* are the people who lived a long time before you.
2 All the ______ in the restaurant turned at the sudden noise.
3 The police are looking for two ______ who were seen running away.

assume drape gossip satisfy summon

4 It was raining and the young man ______ his jacket around the woman's shoulders.
5 Skiing ______ my need to do something exciting every now and again.
6 Mrs Jarvis ______ her son into the living room to explain his behaviour.
7 Your career begins to ______ more importance in your life as you get older.
8 I don't think it's kind to ______ about your friends like that.

elaborate elementary fragrant nomadic primitive wealthy

9 The tribes travel from area to area, so they are ______.
10 The preparations for the wedding were very ______ and took hours.
11 I'm not sure that being ______ makes you happy.
12 The room was full of the ______ smell of roses.
13 The solution to the problem was quite ______ in the end.
14 I don't believe that people are ______ just because they live in the jungle.

B Find words or phrases in the Reading text which have a similar meaning to those below.

1 mixture of different things (paragraph 1) *assortment*
2 importance (paragraph 1) ______
3 important formal event (paragraph 1) ______
4 politeness towards guests (paragraph 2) ______
5 something you must do (paragraph 2) ______
6 social position (paragraph 2) ______
7 something that shows you respect someone (paragraph 2) ______
8 different parts of a meal (paragraph 5) ______
9 circle of flowers (paragraph 6) ______
10 old-fashioned cup (paragraph 6) ______

3 FUTURES

Reading

Student's Book pages 38–39

Wordbank

Vocabulary from the Wordbank on page 39 of the Student's Book

A Rearrange the letters to make a word that fits in each gap.

1 All this vocabulary comes from the Unit 3 Reading ____________ (**BROKDAWN**).
2 We usually take things like electricity and running water for ____________ (**DETRANG**) these days.
3 We've finished the research but we haven't analysed all the ____________ (**TAAD**) yet.
4 It's highly ____________ (**YEKLIL**) that humans will land on Mars within our lifetime.
5 Everyone should try to understand the ____________ (**PENTOCC**) behind Einstein's Theory of Relativity.
6 ____________ (**NEVIG**) that there's no scientific evidence to prove they exist, it's amazing that so many people believe in ghosts.

▸▸▸ *Other vocabulary*

Other vocabulary from the Reading section on pages 38 and 39 of the Student's Book

B Match each word to a word that has a similar meaning.

1 rough	**A** amazing	______
2 immediate	**B** unlikely	______
3 clear	**C** approximate	______
4 improbable	**D** interesting	______
5 thought-provoking	**E** instant	______
6 incredible	**F** obvious	______

C Choose the correct word.

1 If you could go back **on** / **in** time, which era would you choose to go back to?
2 Do you think aliens will ever try to make contact **with** / **to** humans?
3 We have so many means **of** / **for** communication at our disposal these days.
4 You can always rely **on** / **from** this news channel to give you the facts.
5 A small change in the design can make a big difference **in** / **with** practice.
6 You can't break the laws **in** / **of** physics!

D Write one word in each gap.

1 It's a good idea, but it'll never work ____________ reality.
2 Can you make sure the DVD player's connected ____________ the TV properly?
3 Scientists still haven't provided answers ____________ these questions yet.
4 I think you're referring ____________ astrologers rather than astronomers, aren't you?
5 You're not having doubts ____________ the experiment, are you?

6 I'm not aware ___________ any scientific studies which show that telepathy is a real phenomenon.
7 An inch is roughly equivalent ___________ 2.5 centimetres.
8 What are the chances ___________ seeing a shooting star tonight?

E Write a word from below in each gap.

atom benefit consensus encounter objection ~~opponent~~ source

1 Professor Badawi is a major *opponent* of the government's scheme.
2 The general ___________ amongst the scientific community is that climate change is a real phenomenon.
3 The Wikipedia website is a very useful ___________ of information.
4 The number of protons in a/an ___________ determines what chemical element it is.
5 She says that her strange ___________ with an alien creature changed her life forever!
6 My major ___________ to the plan is that it's too expensive.
7 The main ___________ of education is that it enables you to ask the right questions.

F Write the correct form of the word in bold in each gap.

SPACE TOURISM

There are still a large number of (**1**) *unanswered* (**ANSWER**) questions regarding space tourism, particularly to do with the everyday (**2**) ___________ (**PRACTICAL**), such as eating or going to the toilet, of life in space. However, there is widespread (**3**) ___________ (**AGREE**) both within the travel industry and the space technology industry that space tourism is a (**4**) ___________ (**POTENTIAL**) enormous source of income. Although the first space tourists are (**5**) ___________ (**NECESSARY**) extremely wealthy people – and will continue to be for the foreseeable future – the long-term hope is that space tourism will become a (**6**) ___________ (**REAL**) for all of us. In all (**7**) ___________ (**LIKELY**), that is exactly what's going to happen.

Vocabulary boost: phrasal verbs

G Choose the correct word.

1 Can you turn **off** / **out** / **down** the PC when you've finished using it, please?
2 How did you come **off** / **up** / **over** with such a brilliant idea?
3 I screamed when she suddenly turned **into** / **round** / **out** an alien at the end of the film!
4 I'm trying to work **up** / **off** / **out** how many days they've been in space so far.
5 Scientist have narrowed **off** / **down** / **out** the possible landing sites to three options.
6 The design's really come **up** / **on** / **off** since I saw it last. Well done! You're making progress!

Listening

Student's Book page 40

Wordbank

Vocabulary from the Wordbank on page 40 of the Student's Book

A Write one word on each line to replace the words in italics. The first letter is given to help you.

1 It's *not very* surprising that space missions cost billions of dollars. **h**ardly
2 I was worried *at first* that the telescope wouldn't be powerful enough. **i**__________
3 Do astronauts often need to be *helped to remember* to get enough sleep? **r**__________
4 The sizes of distant stars are usually *approximate calculations* because we can't measure them accurately. **e**__________
5 There are no *present* plans to build a space hotel on the Moon. **c**__________

▸▸▸ *Other vocabulary*

Other vocabulary from the Listening section on page 40 of the Student's Book

B The words in italics are in the wrong sentence. Find the correct words and write them on the lines.

1 It takes just over 365 days for the Earth to complete one *galaxy* of the Sun. orbit
2 Our Sun is an average-sized *universe*. __________
3 A/an *orbit* is a group of billions of stars spinning around a central point. __________
4 The galaxy we live in is called the Milky *System*. __________
5 The *star* is all space, and everything that exists within it. __________
6 The planets, including Earth, and the Sun they go around, are known collectively as the Solar *Way*. __________

C Write a word from below in each gap.

Verbs	Nouns	Adjectives
collide merge	agreement collision	close galactic

1 If you want to talk about periods of time in the history of the universe, you can use galactic years.
2 If two objects __________, they hit each other.
3 If there is a/an __________ between two objects, they hit each other.
4 If two organisations or galaxies __________, they join together to form one thing.
5 If two people are in __________, they share the same opinion.
6 If something is __________ to you, it is near you.

Vocabulary boost: word formation

D **Complete the table.**

	Verb	Noun
1	collide	*collision*
2	decide	
3	conclude	
4	permit	
5	invade	
6	admit	
7	persuade	
8	exclude	
9	divide	
10	provide	

E **If a word is spelt correctly, put a tick on the line. If it is spelt incorrectly, rewrite it.**

1 visable ___*visible*___
2 acceptable ____________
3 divisable ____________
4 permissable ____________
5 enjoyable ____________
6 accessable ____________
7 sensable ____________
8 profitable ____________
9 possable ____________
10 valuable ____________
11 horrable ____________
12 responsable ____________
13 admirable ____________
14 flexable ____________
15 disposable ____________

Vocabulary boost: word patterns

F **Change the form of the verb in brackets and add any necessary words to complete the sentences.**

1 I'm not very keen ___*on reading*___ (**READ**) science fiction novels, to be honest.
2 Bad weather prevented the Space Shuttle ____________ (**TAKE OFF**).
3 Are people who wear glasses allowed ____________ (**BECOME**) astronauts?
4 How dare you accuse me ____________ (**NOT KNOW**) how old the Milky Way is!
5 I'm really looking forward ____________ (**SEE**) the new Batman film.
6 Why did they refuse ____________ (**LEAVE**) the spacecraft?
7 I don't deny ____________ (**SEE**) something strange, but I wouldn't say it was definitely a UFO.
8 I don't really approve ____________ (**SPEND**) so much money on space research.
9 Using pencils saved the Soviet Union ____________ (**HAVE**) to invent a pen that worked in zero gravity.

Speaking

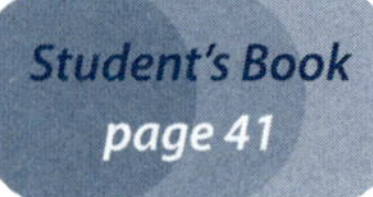

Grammarbank: Talking about the future

Grammar Reference, Section 5, pages 100–101 of the Student's Book

A **If a word or phrase in bold is correct, put a tick. If it's incorrect, rewrite it correctly, including the different possibilities. Use contractions where appropriate.**

1 I don't think **I'll** ever want to live in another country. ______✓______
2 A lot of technology **is becoming** cheaper over the next few years. *will become / is going to become*
3 Do you think people **are living** longer in 100 years' time? ______________
4 **I'm having** a job interview next week, as it happens. ______________
5 When I graduate, **I work** for my dad's company for a while. ______________
6 The course **starts** at the beginning of September. ______________
7 **We don't go** to the planetarium this weekend because we couldn't get tickets. ______________

B **Put each verb into the correct tense, including the different possibilities. Use contractions where appropriate.**

1 He'll have to renew his passport before *he goes* (**HE** / **GO**) abroad to study.
2 I won't know how well I've done in the IELTS exam until ____________ (**I** / **GET**) my results.
3 The engines will stop as soon as the spacecraft ____________ (**LAND**).
4 Remember to keep an eye on the time while ____________ (**YOU** / **DO**) Task 1 of the IELTS Writing module.

C **Write one or two words in each gap.**

1 This time next month, I'll *have* got my IELTS results!
2 What do you think you'll ____________ doing in twenty years?
3 I probably ____________ ____________ heard from the university by the end of February, but they should contact me sometime in March.
4 Perhaps in the future we'll all ____________ ____________ in cities under the sea.

D **CD, 5 Listen to this IELTS candidate answering a question in Part 3 of the Speaking Module. If he uses the verb tense correctly in each phrase, put a tick. If he uses it incorrectly, put a cross and write the reason for your answer on the line.**

1 'there aren't any teachers' *X* *he should have said 'there won't be...'*
2 'the children are going to learn' _____ ______________
3 'children will still have used' _____ ______________
4 'things will have changed' _____ ______________
5 'blackboards will have been replaced' _____ ______________
6 'it will happen' _____ ______________

Wordbank

Vocabulary from the Wordbank on page 41 of the Student's Book

E Write a sentence using the word given so that it has a similar meaning to the sentence before it.

1 There might be life on other planets.
It's possible that there's life on other planets. (POSSIBLE)
2 There's very little chance that it'll snow tomorrow.
____________________ (HIGHLY)
3 We can't know for sure, but maybe there is life after death!
____________________ (IMPOSSIBLE)
4 Our grandchildren may be able to travel round the Solar System.
____________________ (PERHAPS)
5 Do you think UFOs are perhaps secret military planes?
____________________ (MAY)
6 It's not impossible that what you saw was a satellite.
____________________ (POSSIBILITY)
7 The chances of her failing the exam are very low.
____________________ (UNLIKELY)

Vocabulary boost: chance and luck

F Choose the correct word or phrase.

1 I'd love to have the chance **to travel** / **of travelling** round the world.
2 What are the chances **to win** / **of winning** the lottery?
3 There's a small chance **they're going to offer** / **their offering** me the job.
4 If I could study abroad, I'd jump at **the** / **a** chance!
5 She's taking **the** / **a** big chance by setting up her own business.
6 I ran into Doug **with** / **by** chance in the supermarket yesterday.
7 The **chance is** / **chances are** that my IELTS results will come tomorrow!
8 There's a fifty-fifty chance **of** / **for** the match being cancelled.

G Write one word in each gap.

1 *Good* luck with the job interview!
2 You're ________ luck! We've got two tickets left.
3 I'm just calling to ________ you luck in the exam.
4 I couldn't ________ my luck when they told me I'd won the competition.
5 I'd hoped they'd have the shoes in my size, but I was ________ of luck.
6 ________ any luck, we'll be in Shanghai this time next week.

Writing

Student's Book pages 42–43

Grammarbank: Using participles

Grammar Reference, Section 6, page 102 of the Student's Book

A **Choose the correct word or phrase.**

1 While (handling) / **handled** the material, you should always wear gloves.
2 The electricity **producing** / **produced** is stored in a battery.
3 After **examined** / **having examined** the wreckage, the investigator writes a report.
4 **Having** / **Had** large handles, the machine is easy to carry.
5 **Giving** / **Given** the choice, I would prefer the first option.
6 He was the person **driving** / **was driving** the car at the time.
7 **Having seen** / **Seeing** the film once already, I didn't really want to see it again.
8 After **stirred** / **being stirred**, the liquid is poured into a large storage tank.
9 **Having been transferred** / **Having transferred** to a larger container, the mixture is left to cool.

B **Write each verb in the correct form.**

1 *Containing* (**CONTAIN**) bars of gold, the boxes are extremely heavy.
2 ________________ (**TAKE**) to a laboratory, the material is analysed.
3 When ________________ (**ENTER**) the code, the technician uses a special keypad.
4 The steam ________________ (**GIVE OFF**) is used to power a motor.
5 After ________________ (**CHECK**) the brakes, the mechanic checks the tyres.
6 The instrument ________________ (**REGULATE**) the temperature is a thermostat.
7 After ________________ (**PLACE**) on a flat surface, the package is carefully opened.
8 ________________ (**WASH**), the walls are ready to be painted.
9 ________________ (**MAKE**) this dish before, I was confident it would turn out well.

C **Each of these sentences is incorrect because the participle clause has a different subject to the main clause. Rewrite them so the two clauses agree.**

1 Having prepared the equipment, the experiment is started by the research team.
Having prepared the equipment, the research team starts the experiment.
2 After connecting the cables, the equipment is turned on by an operator.
____
3 Wearing a mask, the wood is spray-painted by a skilled technician.
____
4 Looking at the map, the town was six kilometres away.
____
5 Having been assembled, they put the furniture into position.
____

Wordbank

Vocabulary from the Wordbank on page 42 of the Student's Book

D **Choose the correct word.**

1 The second device is slightly smaller **from** / **than** the first one.
2 It is approximately the same size **of** / **as** a mobile phone.
3 It is approximately the size **of** / **as** a mobile phone.
4 The instrument is shaped **like** / **as** a long sharp pencil.
5 The structure of the building is made **from** / **of** steel.
6 The experiment is divided **into** / **by** three different stages.
7 The plans consist **of** / **from** several sets of drawings.
8 The tunnel is cylindrical **in** / **by** shape.

E **Write full sentences.**

1 car – make – aluminium
The car is made of aluminium.
2 process – consist – number of stages
____
3 box – same height – human
____
4 machine – large – car engine
____
5 skyscraper – shape – enormous cigar
____
6 area – divide – four sections
____
7 wings – triangular – shape
____
8 all the furniture – make – wood
____
9 control panel – size – small laptop
____
10 interior – colourful – exterior
____

▸▸▸ Other vocabulary

Other vocabulary from the Writing section on pages 42 and 43 of the Student's Book

F **Match to make phrases.**

1 washing	**5** means of	**A** pilot	**E** aircraft	1D	______
2 mobile	**6** final	**B** transport	**F** phone	______	______
3 automatic	**7** lightweight	**C** plastic	**G** check	______	______
4 light		**D** machine		______	

G **Write one word on each line to replace the word or phrase in italics. The first letter is given to help you.**

1. *When* the batteries have been installed, the equipment is ready to be used. **O**nce________
2. *When* the batteries have been installed, the equipment is ready to be used. **A**____________
3. *A little time* after landing, the plane taxis slowly to the gate. **S**____________
4. At this *point*, the ingredients are mixed together in a large bowl. **s**____________
5. The liquid is pumped into a tank, *in which* it is left to cool. **w**____________

Vocabulary boost: word formation

H **Complete the table. Be careful! Some of the words have irregular forms.**

Adjective	Noun	Verb
1 long	length	elongate ______
2 short	______	______
3 high	______	______
4 low	______	______
5 deep	______	______
6 wide	______	______
7 narrow	______	______
8 large	______	______

I **CD, 6 Listen and complete the table.**

Noun	Adjective	Meaning of adjective
1 size	sizeable	large
2 space	______	having a lot of space inside
3 spot	______	extremely clean
4 substance	______	large in size or amount
5 extend	______	covering a large/wide area
6 signify	______	large, important
7 consider	______	large in size or amount

3 EXAM PRACTICE

Student's Book pages 44–45

Reading

Vocabulary from the Reading text on pages 44 and 45 of the Student's Book

A Find verbs in the Reading text connected to the idea of seeing the future.

1 ___*see into*___ (text title)
2 ________________ (text sub-title)
3 ________________ (text sub-title)
4 ________________ (paragraph C)
5 ________________ (paragraph D)

B Write a word or phrase from below in each gap.

clairvoyance déjà vu gut hunch instinct medium
paradox perception premonition ~~sense~~

1 If you have a sixth ___*sense*___ , you are able to feel or see things without using the normal five senses. (paragraph A)
2 A/An ____________ is a person who claims to be able to communicate with dead people. (paragraph A)
3 If you have extrasensory ____________ , you are able to feel or see things without using the normal five senses. (paragraph A)
4 If you experience ____________ , you have the feeling of repeating a past experience. (paragraph A)
5 ____________ is the ability to see the future or communicate with dead people. (paragraph A)
6 If you have a/an ____________ feeling about something, you think it's true even though you have no evidence. (paragraph A)
7 ____________ is a sense of knowing what to do in a situation. (paragraph A)
8 If you have a/an ____________ , you see something that's going to happen in the future. (paragraph C)
9 If you have a/an ____________ that something is going to happen, you suspect or feel that it might happen, without having any real evidence. (paragraph C)
10 A ____________ is a situation with two aspects which seem to be illogical or opposites. (paragraph E)

C Find adjectives in the Reading text to match these definitions.

1 ___*profound*___ : serious, important (paragraph A)
2 ________________ : beyond what science can explain (paragraph A)
3 ________________ : connected to mysterious mental powers (paragraph A)
4 ________________ : ordinary, everyday, usual (paragraph A)
5 ________________ : very persuasive and convincing (paragraph B)
6 ________________ : strange, odd, unusual (paragraph B)
7 ________________ : with no pattern or planning (paragraph D)
8 ________________ : not changing, steady (paragraph D)
9 ________________ : out-of-date, no longer useable (paragraph E)
10 ________________ : low-quality (paragraph G)

4 ENVIRONMENTS

Reading

Student's Book pages 48–49

Wordbank

Vocabulary from the Wordbank on page 49 of the Student's Book

A Write one word in each gap.

1 Not having a car, and not being able to afford taxis, I rely on ___*public*___ transport to get about.
2 Sir, you were driving at 80 kilometres per hour in an area where the ___________ limit is 50 kilometres per hour.
3 The new ___________ energy lightbulbs use a lot less electricity than the old ones.
4 All the furniture is made from ___________ materials; all the wood and plastic fittings come from old pieces of furniture.
5 It's very difficult to find ___________ housing round here; most of the properties are far too expensive for us.
6 ___________ disposal isn't just about rubbish – it's also how you get rid of dirty water and sewage.
7 No car is 100% ___________ friendly, but electric cars do a lot less damage than petrol and diesel ones.
8 All company flights have to be ___________ neutral, so for every 1,000 miles we fly, the company pays for a certain number of trees to be planted.

Other vocabulary

Other vocabulary from the Reading section on pages 48 and 49 of the Student's Book

B Write a word from below in each gap.

cost-effective   efficient   essential   ~~picturesque~~
reliable   rural   suburban   urban

1 With its lovely little square and the mountains in the background, it's one of the most ___*picturesque*___ small towns I've ever visited.
2 It's ___________ that we start thinking about alternatives to oil as it's going to run out one day.
3 I grew up on a pig farm, so it was a very ___________ way of life.
4 Flying business class may be more comfortable, but it's just not ___________ for a small company like this; the tickets are extremely expensive.
5 This car does get through a lot of petrol but at least it's ___________ – it hasn't broken down once in ten years.
6 I live in the city centre, so it's about as ___________ an environment as it's possible to get!
7 As a secretary, you've got to be very ___________ otherwise the office can become completely disorganised.
8 We live in a very ___________ area, which is great because we're not too far from the city centre, and not that far from the countryside either.

C **Write a verb from below in the correct form in each gap.**

adhere   aim   anticipate   aspire   assume   ~~bloom~~   draw up   fine

1 How often do these flowers ___bloom___ ?
2 Jess Reece, aged 19, ___________ £200 yesterday for speeding in a built-up area.
3 It's extremely important that the fire safety regulations ___________ to.
4 The advertising campaign ___________ particularly at teenagers.
5 New guidelines ___________ recently, which will be published shortly.
6 Most government ministers ___________ to be Prime Minister.
7 I ___________ you were joking when you said you were moving to Mexico.
8 It ___________ that a large number of people will attend the public meeting.

Vocabulary boost: phrasal verbs

D **Choose the correct word.**

1 If the weather clears **away** / (**up**), we can go hiking tomorrow, if you like.
2 It's so foggy that it's difficult to make **out** / **off** where the side of the road is.
3 Let's wait till the storm dies **down** / **over** a bit before leaving.
4 Don't throw those newspapers **off** / **away** – they can be recycled!
5 How long did it take for them to put the forest fire **down** / **out**?
6 Living on an island, we get completely cut **off** / **out** from the mainland during bad weather.
7 They're doing **up** / **over** a lot of the old warehouses and turning them into flats.

Vocabulary boost: word formation

E **Write the correct form of the word in bold in each gap.**

1 With there being only several thousand left on the whole planet, the Giant Panda is a/an ___endangered___ (**DANGER**) species.
2 A number of animals such as the Giant Panda face ______________ (**EXTINCT**) unless more is done to protect them.
3 The hurricane caused widespread ______________ (**DESTROY**).
4 Everyone knows everyone else in my ______________ (**NEIGHBOUR**).
5 I don't mind the ______________ (**LIGHT**); it's the thunder I don't like!
6 Animals brought up in zoos can't easily be released back into their natural ______________ (**SURROUND**).
7 ______________ (**INDUSTRY**) waste is a major source of pollution in rivers and seas.
8 Don't worry! The dog's quite ______________ (**HARM**). He won't bite you!
9 We live in a built-up ______________ (**RESIDE**) area.
10 What's your ______________ (**EXPLAIN**) for climate change if it's not caused by humans?

Listening

Student's Book page 50

Wordbank

Vocabulary from the Wordbank on page 50 of the Student's Book

A Write a word from the Wordbank on each line to replace the words in italics.

1 Air Krash is not a very *appropriate* name for an airline, is it? ___apt___
2 The state of Hawaii is not physically connected to *the mainland of the* USA. ____________
3 The plant-life is really *green and healthy* on this part of the island. ____________
4 Look at that *enormous* iceberg! ____________
5 India and Bangladesh experience a powerful *heavy and continuous rain* every six months. ____________
6 With temperatures falling to minus 60 degrees at night, the place is extremely *difficult to live in* in the winter. ____________

Other vocabulary

Other vocabulary from the Listening section on page 50 of the Student's Book

B Rearrange the letters to make a word that fits the gap.

1 The airport's in a ___valley___ (**YALEVL**) between two high mountains.
2 The Empire State Building in New York was the world's tallest ____________ (**REPAKYSSRC**) for more than forty years.
3 The ____________ (**MANICKNE**) for New York State is 'the Empire State'.
4 Let's climb over that sand ____________ (**NEUD**) and see what's on the other side.
5 Mountainous regions are often known as ____________ (**SINDHGLAH**).
6 There's very little ____________ (**NOTAGEVETI**) in Antarctica.
7 There's less than a centimetre of rainfall ____________ (**REP**) year, on average.
8 Did you know that approximately 90% of people live in the ____________ (**RENTHORN**) hemisphere?

Vocabulary boost: measurements

C Write the abbreviations for these measurements.

1 five millimetres ___5 mm___
2 ten centimetres ____________
3 four and a half metres ____________
4 seven square metres ____________
5 twenty-one grams ____________
6 two kilograms ____________
7 ten tonnes ____________
8 two and a quarter litres ____________
9 fifty kilometres per hour ____________
10 eighteen degrees Celsius/Centigrade ____________

D **Answer the questions.**

1 How many millimetres are there in a centimetre? ___10___
2 How many centimetres are there in a metre? ______
3 How many grams are there in a kilogram? ______
4 How many kilograms are there in a tonne? ______
5 Is 'area' measured in m^2 or m^3? ______
6 Is 'volume' measured in m^2 or m^3? ______
7 At what temperature does water freeze? ______
8 At what temperature does water boil? ______

E **Write a word from below in each gap to complete the table. Use a dictionary if necessary.**

Fahrenheit feet gallons inches ~~miles~~
pints pounds stones tonnes yards

In some countries, they use...	instead of...
(**1**) ___miles___	kilometres
(**2**) ______	centimetres
(**3**) ______ and (**4**) ______	metres
(**5**) ______ and (**6**) ______	kilograms
(**7**) ______ and (**8**) ______	litres
(**9**) ______	tons
(**10**) ______	Celsius or Centigrade

F **CD, 7 Have a guess! Write a number in each gap in the first column. Then listen and write the actual number in the second column.**

	My guess	The actual number
(**1**) The number of centimetres in an inch	___3___	___2.54___
(**2**) The number of inches in a foot	______	______
(**3**) The number of feet in a yard	______	______
(**4**) The number of centimetres in a yard	______	______
(**5**) The number of yards in a mile	______	______
(**6**) The number of metres in a mile	______	______

Speaking

Student's Book page 51

Grammarbank: Using countable and uncountable nouns / articles

Grammar Reference, Section 7, pages 102–103 of the Student's Book

A Write the nouns in the correct column.

advice ~~book~~ ~~chocolate~~ ~~clothes~~ fact furniture glass groceries hair housework information jeans job knowledge ~~luggage~~ money news paper programme scissors sheep suitcase time trousers work

Always countable	Always singular uncountable	Always plural uncountable	Both countable and uncountable depending on meaning
book	*luggage*	*clothes*	*chocolate*
______	______	______	______
______	______	______	______
______	______	______	______
______	______	______	______
______	______	______	______
______	______	______	______
______	______	______	______
______	______	______	______

B Choose the correct word or phrase.

1 **(Is)/ Are** there a lot of money in the account?
2 **Is / Are** the scissors in the kitchen drawer?
3 The glass in these glasses **is / are** photo-chromatic.
4 How **much / many** times did I ask you to book the tickets?

C Write 'a', 'an' or 'the' in each gap. If no article is necessary, put a dash (–).

SEOUL

(1) *The* city of **(2)** ______ Seoul lies in **(3)** ______ north west of **(4)** ______ South Korea, approximately 50 kilometres from **(5)** ______ North Korean border. With **(6)** ______ population of almost 23 million, **(7)** ______ Seoul National Capital Area is **(8)** ______ world's second largest metropolitan area. **(9)** ______ area includes **(10)** ______ Seoul itself, together with **(11)** ______ port of Incheon and **(12)** ______ various other satellite towns. Designated as **(13)** ______ 'Special City', of which there are several throughout North and South Korea, the SNCA is administered by **(14)** ______ South Korea's government. Seoul is **(15)** ______ international financial centre, and has hosted **(16)** ______ several global sporting events, including **(17)** ______ 1988 Summer Olympics and **(18)** ______ 2002 FIFA World Cup. **(19)** ______ history of Seoul can be traced back to **(20)** ______ 18 BC.

D **Write 'few' or 'little' in each gap. Then choose the meaning of the sentence from the words and phrases in bold.**

1. They only gave me a ___*little*___ information about the island.
   They gave me some / (**They didn't give me a lot of**) information.
2. They gave me ________________ news about what had happened.
   They gave me some / **They didn't give me a lot of** news.
3. A ________________ plants grow here.
   Some / **Not a lot of** plants grow here.
4. Only a ________________ guides will take you there.
   Some / **Not a lot of** guides will take you there.
5. They gave me a ________________ advice before the trip.
   They gave me some / **They didn't give me much** advice.
6. ________________ people have managed to climb to the top.
   Some / **Not many** people have managed it.

Wordbank

Vocabulary from the Wordbank on page 51 of the Student's Book

E **Choose the correct word.**

1. Do you prefer living in the country (**to**) / **than** life in the city?
2. I'd rather go somewhere quieter **to** / **than** stay here, to be honest.
3. I'd rather we **not** / **didn't** go by bus, if you don't mind.
4. I think I'd **prefer** / **rather** to build my own house, if I could.
5. I'd **prefer** / **rather** they hadn't stayed so long, but never mind.
6. **Do** / **Would** you prefer to have lived in ancient Egypt or ancient Greece?

F **Write one word in each gap.**

1. I'd rather ___*not*___ live somewhere quite so far from a supermarket.
2. ____________ you prefer to meet at six tomorrow night ____________ than seven?
3. ____________ you rather we ____________ go on a cruise again this year?
4. I generally prefer ____________ to drive in the dark.
5. ____________ you generally prefer travelling by bus or train?
6. I'd ____________ they ____________ phoned us first instead of just turning up!

Vocabulary boost: phrases with 'go'

G **CD, 8 Choose the correct word or phrase. Then listen and check your answers.**

1. go (**home**) / **to home**
2. go **bed** / **to bed**
3. go **for work** / **to work**
4. go **for a swim** / **for swimming**
5. go **abroad** / **to abroad**
6. go **for camping** / **camping**
7. go **sightseeing** / **for sightseeing**
8. go **on a tour** / **for a tour**
9. go **by train/bus** / **on train/bus**
10. go **by foot** / **on foot**

Writing

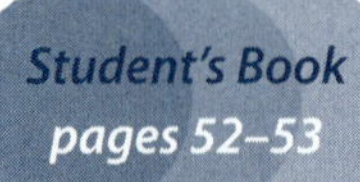
Student's Book pages 52–53

Grammarbank: Using modals

Grammar Reference, Section 8, pages 103–104 of the Student's Book

A **Choose the correct word or phrase.**

1 In my opinion, the government **ought** / **should** ban factories from polluting the atmosphere.
2 Working in a coal mine **must** / **should** be an extremely demanding and dangerous job.
3 The oil tanker **mustn't** / **can't** have spilled its oil on purpose; it **must** / **can** have been an accident.
4 Everyone **has** / **must** to make an effort to be more environmentally responsible.
5 We do not know for certain, but the ancient city **can** / **could** have been destroyed by a tsunami.
6 **Do you need** / **Need you** to take the bottles to be recycled, or are they collected?
7 Antarctica **shouldn't** / **couldn't** always have been covered in ice; tropical plants used to grow there.

B **Write the correct form of the verb in each gap. Be careful! Some verbs might not change form.**

1 We ought *to get* (**GET**) a guide book before we go on holiday.
2 We should ____________ (**BUY**) a guide book before we went on holiday.
3 There must ____________ (**BE**) at least 500 people at last night's meeting.
4 The hotel was nice, but it shouldn't ____________ (**BUILD**) so far from the sea.
5 Who knows what might ____________ (**HAPPEN**) if they discover a large meteor heading towards Earth?
6 Who knows what might ____________ (**HAPPEN**) if dinosaurs hadn't become extinct?
7 Did you have ____________ (**HAVE**) a tour guide, or could you ____________ (**LOOK**) round on your own?
8 You could ____________ (**ARREST**) if they'd caught you there without permission.

C **Rewrite each sentence using the word in bold.**

1 That almost certainly wasn't the right turning. **HAVE**
That can't have been the right turning.
2 I'm almost certain we made a mistake. **HAVE**
____
3 It would be a good idea for the council to renovate the old mill. **OUGHT**
____
4 You were wrong to buy a car that uses so much petrol. **SHOULDN'T**
____
5 If you have a solar-powered water heater, you aren't forced to use electricity to heat the water. **NEED**
____

Wordbank

Vocabulary from the Wordbank on page 52 of the Student's Book

D Write one word in each gap.

1 In *spite* of the cost, it would certainly be sensible for governments to invest in nuclear power.
2 ____________ said ____________, we should not forget that there have been accidents at nuclear power stations in the past.
3 ____________ contrast, wind-generated power is extremely safe and clean.
4 On ____________ other ____________, an enormous number of wind turbines are required to produce only a small amount of power.
5 ____________ though electric cars have been developed, very few have been sold.
6 Even ____________ we all stopped polluting the atmosphere tomorrow, the hole in the ozone layer would still exist.
7 ____________ having gas installed, we still use a lot of electricity.
8 ____________ I agree we should all try to be carbon neutral, I recognise it is very difficult in practice.

▸▸▸ *Other vocabulary*

Other vocabulary from the Writing section on pages 52 and 53 of the Student's Book

E Match to make phrases. If more than one phrase is possible, write all of the possibilities.

1	firm	A	phenomena	*1H, F*
2	widely-held	B	activity	______
3	natural	C	option	______
4	human	D	energy	______
5	solar	E	travel	______
6	air	F	view	______
7	alternative	G	radiation	______
8	realistic	H	evidence	______

F Write one word in each gap so the sentences have the same meaning.

1 The locations of the 5 new eco-towns have not been finalised yet.
  a When choosing the best location for a new eco-town, a large number of factors have to be *considered*.
  b When choosing the best location for a new eco-town, a large number of factors have to be ____________ into account.

2 An annual ceremony is held to remember the victims of the fire.
  a It usually ____________ on the first of January.
  b It usually takes ____________ on the first of January.

3 Coal from other parts of the world is cheaper than home-produced coal.
   a As a ____________, most British coal mines have closed in the past 30 years.
   b For this ____________, most British coal mines have closed in the past 30 years.

4 One alternative energy source which should be developed is wind power.
   a In the ____________ way, further research should be done into wave power.
   b ____________, further research should be done into wave power.

5 I agree we should all try to be carbon neutral.
   a ____________, I recognise it is very difficult in practice.
   b ____________, I recognise it is very difficult in practice.

G Choose the correct word.

1 Some scientists **disagree** / (**dispute**) the findings.
2 I don't really **approve** / **agree** of governments **saying** / **telling** people how to behave.
3 Parking is not **accepted** / **permitted** in this area between 9 am and 5 pm.
4 Do you **deny** / **challenge** that the polar ice caps are melting?
5 The scientist **told** / **confessed** that he had manipulated his results.
6 We all have to **comprehend** / **recognise** the fact that we share this planet with other species.
7 Reading that environmental report has made me **dispute** / **question** my own behaviour.
8 I **challenge** / **question** you to provide evidence to support your views.
9 It's difficult to **comprehend** / **argue** how big a problem this really is.
10 Not being experts ourselves, we often have to **agree** / **trust** and **accept** / **approve** the opinions of experts.

Vocabulary boost: word formation

H Complete the table.

Verb	Noun	
1 accept		*acceptance*
2 acknowledge		____________
3 agree	Positive: ____________	Negative: ____________
4 approve	Positive: ____________	Negative: ____________
5 challenge		____________
6 comprehend	Positive: ____________	Negative: ____________
7 confess		____________
8 deny		____________
9 dispute		____________
10 permit		____________
11 recognise		____________
12 trust	Positive: ____________	Negative: ____________

4

EXAM PRACTICE

Student's Book pages 54–55

Reading

Vocabulary from the Reading text on pages 54 and 55 of the Student's Book

A Match each noun to the correct definition.

1	shard (text sub-title)	A	wild area of land untouched by humans	1F
2	peninsula (paragraph A)	B	large piece	____
3	glacier (paragraph B)	C	peacefulness	____
4	wilderness (paragraph B)	D	strip of land sticking out into water	____
5	chunk (paragraph B)	E	main idea	____
6	sediment (paragraph C)	F	sharp piece	____
7	serenity (paragraph C)	G	very large sheet of ice that slowly moves	____
8	thrust (paragraph D)	H	attacks causing damage and destruction	____
9	ravages (paragraph D)	I	substance that settles at the bottom of a liquid	____

B Choose the best definition for each adjective.

1 weather-pummelled (paragraph A): **attacked** / **protected** by the weather
2 subtle (paragraph B): **obvious, loud and simple** / **not obvious but quiet and clever**
3 jagged (paragraph B): **flat and smooth** / **rough and sharp**
4 translucent (paragraph C): **clear** / **not clear** enough for light to pass through
5 scarce (paragraph D): **rare** / **common**
6 radical (paragraph D): **obvious** / **extreme**
7 reflective (paragraph E): **thoughtful** / **colourful**
8 aquatic (paragraph F): involving or connected to **water** / **art**
9 aesthetic (paragraph G): **unpleasant** / **pleasant** to look at

C Write a verb from the text in the correct form in each gap to complete the definitions.

1 to *overlook* (paragraph A): have a view of
2 to ____________ (paragraph B): give someone enthusiasm to create something
3 to ____________ (paragraph C): move away, disappear
4 to ____________ (paragraph C): make loud, wild or angry noises
5 to ____________ (paragraph D): change from a solid to a liquid
6 to ____________ (paragraph E): work together
7 to ____________ (paragraph E): take apart, take to pieces
8 to ____________ (paragraph E): give, usually for a particular use or cause
9 to ____________ (paragraph E): pay for, support financially

REVIEW UNITS 1–4

A **Choose the correct answer.**

1 Could you ____________ me a favour?
A make **B** do **C** give **D** take

2 There's been a ____________ increase in unemployment recently.
A sharp **B** pointed **C** strict **D** loud

3 What's the speed ____________ on motorways in your country?
A border **B** limit **C** boundary **D** edge

4 ____________ students make up 40% of the total student population.
A Remote **B** Distant **C** Abroad **D** Overseas

5 Do you think taxis are a public or private ____________ of transport?
A styles **B** methods **C** means **D** ways

6 Sculpture is an art ____________ which has never really interested me.
A form **B** type **C** sort **D** shape

7 I'm really looking ____________ to seeing Matt again on Saturday.
A ahead **B** before **C** further **D** forward

8 I always ____________ my health for granted until I became ill.
A did **B** made **C** put **D** took

8 marks

B **Write the correct form of the word in bold in each gap.**

WOLFGANG AMADEUS MOZART

While there is no doubt that Mozart is one of the most famous and talented (**1**) ____________ (**MUSIC**) the world has ever known, there are still many (**2**) ____________ (**ANSWER**) questions surrounding his death in 1791. There is no (**3**) ____________ (**AGREE**) about the symptoms of Mozart's final illness. The swelling in his hands and feet, and the pain he felt, were all (**4**) ____________ (**ACCURATE**) recorded at the time. However, there is much (**5**) ____________ (**CONFUSE**) regarding the cause of his symptoms. What disease or condition did Mozart die of? One theory is that Mozart was poisoned by fellow composer Antonio Salieri. This story (**6**) ____________ (**ORIGIN**) shortly after Mozart died, and Salieri suffered greatly from the accusations. Because so much time has passed since Mozart's death, it is (**7**) ____________ (**POSSIBLE**) to say with absolutely (**8**) ____________ (**CERTAIN**) exactly what happened. In all (**9**) ____________ (**LIKELY**), however, Mozart died of (**10**) ____________ (**NATURE**) causes – most probably rheumatic fever.

10 marks

C **Rewrite each sentence, starting with the words given.**

1 Mrs Johnson gave the students their exam results.
The students ____.

2 The last time I went to Dubai was in 2006.
I haven't ____.

3 I didn't wake up on time despite setting my alarm clock.
In spite ____.

4 In my opinion, the advantages far outweigh the disadvantages.
As far ____.

5 It's possible that there'll be a storm later today.
There ______________________________ .

6 She wrote the essay and then checked it carefully.
Having ______________________________ .

7 I'm sure it wasn't easy for you to organise the event on your own.
It can't ______________________________ .

8 I'm almost certain we took the wrong turning back there.
We must ______________________________ .

8 marks

D Write one word in each gap.

1 I can't wait till Amy Winehouse's new CD comes ____________ !
2 Let's try and narrow ____________ the options so we've only got two or three.
3 I get ____________ really well with my manager – she's more like a friend than a boss.
4 MP3 players have really caught ____________ recently – now everyone's got one.
5 The government's bringing ____________ a law banning smoking in public.
6 They'll have to draw ____________ some fire safety guidelines for the new building.
7 I've got to buy some paint today to do ____________ the spare bedroom.
8 I'm trying to work ____________ how much money the holiday's going to cost in total.

8 marks

E Choose the correct word.

1 Are you capable **of** / **for** holding your breath underwater for more than a minute?
2 You shouldn't have accused her **for** / **of** stealing without any evidence.
3 I've come **to** / **at** the conclusion that success isn't just about earning lots of money.
4 I really hope you succeed **in** / **to** persuading Adam to come with us.
5 You can always rely **for** / **on** Sabirah – she won't let you down.
6 Do you really prefer staying in **to** / **from** going out?
7 Shall we take the car or are we going **by** / **on** foot?
8 Why would aliens want to make contact **with** / **at** humans?

8 marks

F Write a word from below in each gap.

audience famine fortnight funds nickname objection opponent valley

1 Mr Singh's away on holiday for the next ____________ .
2 The company just hasn't got the ____________ to expand at the moment.
3 Sara's a strong ____________ of the road-widening scheme.
4 Was Jonathon's ____________ at school really 'Jake'?
5 With no rain for two years, it's hardly surprising the region's facing a serious ____________ .
6 The comedian brought four members of the ____________ up on stage.
7 The river at the bottom of the ____________ is perfect for white-water rafting.
8 I've got no ____________ to Terry taking tomorrow off – have you?

8 marks

Total score: _____ / 50

SCIENCES

Reading

Student's Book pages 58–59

Wordbank

Vocabulary from the Wordbank on page 59 of the Student's Book

A **Rearrange the letters to make a word that fits in the gap.**

1 We need to find more evidence to *confirm* (**ROMNFIC**) the theory.
2 Do you think they should build more reactors to produce ___________ (**ELRAUNC**) power?
3 The idea of atoms ___________ (**IANTEDORIG**) in the work of Democritus in ancient Greece.
4 Water is composed of two ___________ (**STEEELNM**): hydrogen and oxygen.
5 It has been ___________ (**ALLTADUCEC**) that about 9,100 stars are visible with the naked eye.
6 Mars ___________ (**RISOTB**) the Sun in a period of 687 days.

Other vocabulary

Other vocabulary from the Reading section on pages 58 and 59 of the Student's Book

B **Match each word or phrase to the correct definition.**

exoplanet ~~planet~~ Solar System supernova

1 *planet* : one of the very large objects like the Earth that go around the Sun
2 ___________ : an exploding star which can be seen in the night sky
3 ___________ : the Sun and all the objects that go around it
4 ___________ : a very large object that goes around a distant star

brightness mass position

5 ___________ : exact location of an object
6 ___________ : amount of light produced or reflected by an object
7 ___________ : weight of an object

carbon helium hydrogen iron

8 ___________ : a chemical element found in coal and diamonds
9 ___________ : a light gas sometimes used as a fuel
10 ___________ : a common metal used in steel to make cars, etc.
11 ___________ : a light gas sometimes used to fill balloons

C **Write the verbs from below in the correct form in each gap.**

convert demote ~~enter~~ expand

1 We *are entering/were entering/have entered* a very exciting period in space exploration.
2 As you put gas into the balloon, it ______________ because of the pressure.
3 How do you ______________ miles into kilometres?
4 As we have learned more about the universe, the Sun has been ______________ in importance.

Vocabulary boost: word formation

D **Each of these verbs forms a noun ending in *-ion*. Write the nouns.**

1 accuse *accusation*
2 apply ______________
3 calculate ______________
4 convert ______________
5 destroy ______________
6 erode ______________
7 expand ______________
8 expect ______________
9 observe ______________
10 produce ______________
11 recognise ______________
12 solve ______________

E **Write a noun from Exercise D in the correct form in each gap.**

1 Even with the naked eye, *observations* of Mars show that it's a dark red colour.
2 I don't accept the ______________ that exploring space is a waste of money.
3 He won the Nobel Prize in ______________ of his work on nuclear power.
4 The valley was created by a process of ______________ over millions of years.
5 We didn't have any ______________ that we would find life on the planet, but we did!
6 The ______________ of the ozone layer is perhaps the biggest problem facing us today.
7 I'm pleased to inform you that your ______________ to study medicine has been successful.
8 I'm sure we'll find a ______________ to the problem if we try hard enough.

Vocabulary boost: elements

F **Match each word to the correct description.**

1	aluminium	A	a soft, heavy metal, used in weights	*1C*
2	chlorine	B	a gas which makes up 78% of the atmosphere	______
3	copper	C	a light metal, used to make saucepans	______
4	gold	D	a gas in the atmosphere which we need to breathe	______
5	lead	E	a hard element, used to make computer chips	______
6	mercury	F	a valuable yellow metal, used in jewellery	______
7	nitrogen	G	a brown metal, used in electrical wires	______
8	oxygen	H	a liquid metal, used in thermometers	______
9	silicon	I	a valuable grey metal, used in jewellery	______
10	silver	J	a green gas, often added to the water in swimming pools	______

Listening

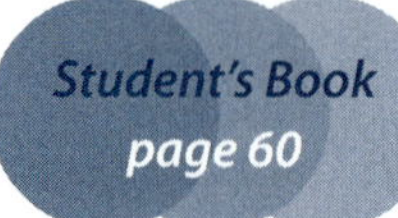

Wordbank

Vocabulary from the Wordbank on page 60 of the Student's Book

A Write a word from the Wordbank in each gap. The first letter of each word is given to help you.

1 Now we've got **w***i-fi*________, I can use my laptop anywhere in the house.
2 Scientists **e**__________ that the universe is about 14 billion years old.
3 A 'flash drive' is a **d**__________ that stores computer files.
4 My computer seems to take a very long time to **b**__________ up.
5 It amazes me that some people lack even an **e**__________ understanding of physics.

▸▸▸ Other vocabulary

Other vocabulary from the Listening section on page 60 of the Student's Book

B Write a word or phrase from below in each gap.

compass needle tissue paper ~~bowl~~ magnet ball bearing

1 A __*bowl*__ is a kind of deep dish.
2 A __________ is a piece of metal that is attracted to other pieces of metal.
3 A __________ is a small round piece of metal, used in machines.
4 __________ is very thin and is used for wrapping things.
5 A __________ is made of metal and is used for sewing.
6 A __________ tells you which way north is.

C Write a word or phrase from Exercise B in each gap.

1 There's a hole in my jumper! Can you pass me that __*needle*__ and cotton?
2 When we moved house, I used __________ to stop things breaking when I packed.
3 I usually start the day with a cup of coffee and a __________ of cornflakes.
4 I always take a __________ with me when I go camping so I don't get lost.
5 I opened up part of the machine and hundreds of __________ rolled out.
6 They use a huge __________ to separate the metal from all the other rubbish.

Vocabulary boost: phrasal verbs

D CD, 9 Write one word in each gap. Then listen and check your answers.

1 plug __*in*__ : connect to the electricity supply
2 switch _____ : start a machine working
3 break _____ : (for a machine, car, etc.) stop working

4 find ______ : discover (information, etc.)
5 come ______ with: think of (an idea, a plan, etc.)
6 carry ______ : perform (an experiment, repairs, etc.)

E **Write a phrasal verb from Exercise D in the correct form in each gap.**

1 They are working on a way of charging mobiles without the need to ___*plug*___ them ___*in*___ .
2 The government is planning to ______________ a study into alternative sources of energy.
3 My car ______________ in the middle of nowhere and I had to walk to a garage.
4 Who first ______________ the idea of using a mouse to control a computer?
5 I ______________ the TV and caught the end of the news report about the explosion.
6 We should ______________ the results of the experiment by the end of the week.

Vocabulary boost: word patterns

F **Write a word from below in each gap. You need to use one word more than once.**

for from in of on

1 to apologise _*for*_ something
2 to believe ______ something
3 to approve ______ something
4 to be proud ______ something
5 to benefit ______ something
6 to comment ______ something

G **Choose the correct word.**

1 to convince somebody **on** / (**of**) something
2 to depend **on** / **from** something
3 to insist **for** / **on** something
4 to object **to** / **about** something
5 to rely **with** / **on** something
6 to be responsible **for** / **from** something

H **Write the correct form of a phrase from Exercises F and G in each gap.**

1 Ben _*insisted on*_ coming with us, even though we didn't really want him to.
2 Being in charge of the experiment meant I __________ checking the results.
3 Whether the experiment goes ahead or not __________ the weather.
4 The scientist __________ misleading the scientific community.
5 Professor Wang was very __________ his achievements.
6 We need to __________ the government __________ the need to act now.
7 Many people __________ experiments on animals and say it's cruel.
8 Do you __________ the search for scientific truth, whatever the consequences?
9 If I'm right, the whole world could __________ my research.
10 Every scientist has to __________ assistants to help in their research.
11 She refused to __________ reports that life had been discovered on Mars.
12 I don't __________ research into nuclear weapons and think it should be banned.

Speaking

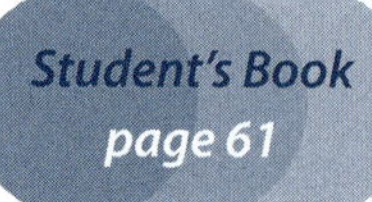

Grammarbank: Using verbs + -ing/infinitives

Grammar Reference, Section 9, pages 104–105 of the Student's Book

A Write the verbs in the correct column. Some verbs may go in more than one column.

~~admit~~ afford allow cause choose consider deny encourage
enjoy fail hope intend let like make manage mind
offer plan refuse risk suggest tell tend wish

+ *-ing*	+ full infinitive	+ object + full infinitive	+ object + bare infinitive
admit			

B Write the correct form of the word in bold in each gap.

SCIENCE AS A CAREER

Many young people enjoy (**1**) *studying* (**STUDY**) science at school and decide (**2**) ___________ (**PURSUE**) it as a career. Those who manage (**3**) ___________ (**FOLLOW**) a career in the sciences find that it allows them (**4**) ___________ (**SATISFY**) their intellectual curiosity. However, if you are considering (**5**) ___________ (**APPLY**) for a university course in a science subject, you should bear in mind that most sciences are very competitive. There will be lots of other people hoping (**6**) ___________ (**SUCCEED**) in your chosen field, and you can't afford (**7**) ___________ (**RELAX**) until you've established a reputation for yourself.

If you intend (**8**) ___________ (**BECOME**) a scientist, then it helps if you don't mind (**9**) ___________ (**WORK**) hard. Even after qualifying, you will find that you are a junior member of a team, being told what (**10**) ___________ (**DO**) by more senior scientists. However, if you choose (**11**) ___________ (**COMMIT**) yourself fully to your dream and can find people to work with who encourage you (**12**) ___________ (**STICK**) with it, then who knows? You may just find yourself with a Nobel Prize one day.

C Choose the correct word or phrase.

1 As I was walking to my lecture, I stopped **buying** / **to buy** a notebook.
2 Did you remember **checking** / **to check** the results?
3 Why don't you try **asking** / **to ask** Paul what he did in the same situation?
4 I'll never forget **meeting** / **to meet** Stephen Hawking, the famous physicist.
5 I wish you would stop **saying** / **to say** that there's no proof for evolution.
6 Do you regret **quitting** / **to quit** your course?
7 Please don't forget **sending** / **to send** your paper to Dr Jones.
8 I've been trying **ringing** / **to ring** you all morning but there was no answer.

Wordbank

Vocabulary from the Wordbank on page 61 of the Student's Book

D Write one word in each gap.

I've always been interested in science, and I'm planning to follow a career in astronomy. I find learning about the planets really interesting. Another interesting (**1**) ___aspect___ of it is that you get to study the history of the universe. As (**2**) ____________ as that, there's the chance that you might discover something useful for mankind. It's also (**3**) ____________ pointing out that you can make a good living in astronomy if you're successful. I'd also (**4**) ____________ to add that I think more people should study science subjects. Most people don't understand very much about science and it's important because we spend a lot of money on scientific research. In (**5**) ____________ to that, we need to be able to control what scientists do and we can only do that if we understand their work. A (**6**) ____________ point is that knowing more about science enriches your life.

Vocabulary boost: phrases

E Write a verb from below in each gap. You need to use some verbs more than once.

give have make pay play take

1 ___have/take___ control of something
2 ____________ attention to something
3 ____________ an effect on something
4 ____________ something for granted
5 ____________ someone the impression that
6 ____________ up your mind about something
7 ____________ a mistake
8 ____________ a role in something

F Write the correct form of a phrase from Exercise E in each gap.

1 If you ___pay attention to___ your tutors, I'm sure you'll manage to understand the course.
2 Have you ________________ whether you're going to do a science degree or not?
3 The Earth's orbit creates seasons which ________________ the weather all over the planet.
4 You shouldn't ________________ success in these exams ________________. You need to revise.
5 Kwan ________________ me ________________ that he was confident his experiment would succeed.
6 I suddenly realised I had ________________ in my calculations.
7 You need to ________________ your life and decide exactly what you want to achieve.
8 Do you think your genes ________________ in the kind of person you become?

Writing

Student's Book pages 62–63

Grammarbank: Using relative clauses

Grammar Reference, Section 10, page 105 of the Student's Book

A **Write a word from below in each gap. You need to use some words more than once. When there is more than one correct answer, write all the possible answers.**

that when where which who whose why

1 The person *who/that* I admire the most is the inventor, Thomas Edison.
2 The reason ____________ science is important is that it helps us understand the world.
3 Natural selection, ____________ was an idea developed by Charles Darwin, is still controversial.
4 Yale, ____________ I studied, has world class research facilities.
5 One question ____________ scientists have yet to solve is how life started.
6 Albert Einstein, ____________ ideas revolutionised science, was born in 1879.
7 The day ____________ we landed on the moon was a day I shall never forget.
8 This is the very room ____________ nitrogen was first discovered.

B **In some sentences there is an extra word. Cross the extra word out. If a sentence is correct, put a tick.**

1 Medical science, which ~~it~~ is one of the most popular courses, lasts four years. ______
2 The course which I applied for was cancelled, which it was very annoying. ______
3 Maths, which I did badly in at school, is now a big part of my working life. ______
4 Tony, who he was planning to be an engineer, failed all his exams. ______
5 The reason that I chose to study here was the fees, which they are quite low. ______
6 There's a woman on my course who she is brilliant at maths. ______

C **Rewrite each pair of sentences as one sentence using a relative clause. If there are different ways of answering, write them too.**

1 One of the men is talking. He is my physics teacher.
The man *who (that) is talking is my physics teacher.*
2 Iron conducts electricity. Its chemical symbol is Fe.
Iron ____.
3 I saw a documentary. It explained how magnets work.
I saw ____.
4 Dr Carlisle was an expert in genetics. He has died.
Dr Carlisle ____.
5 Hydrogen explodes easily. It used to be used in airships.
Hydrogen ____.
6 I found an article. It was all about working in science.
I found ____.

Wordbank

Vocabulary from the Wordbank on page 62 of the Student's Book

D Write the correct form of the word in bold in each gap.

1 The most ___*significant*___ (**SIGNIFY**) feature of the data is the sharp drop over the last five years.
2 It's very __________ (**NOTICE**) that the figure has more than doubled in two years.
3 A __________ (**CENTRE**) feature of the graph is that it has remained steady for a decade.
4 The most __________ (**PROMINENCE**) aspect of the chart is the increase in recent years.
5 One __________ (**STRIKE**) feature is that the number has dropped to almost zero recently.
6 The most __________ (**ESSENCE**) feature is the sudden rise in numbers since 2005.

Other vocabulary

Other vocabulary from the Writing section on pages 62 and 63 of the Student's Book

E Match each word to the correct definition.

1	laboratory	A	the science which studies living things	*1E*
2	biology	B	the science which studies elements and how they react	____
3	physics	C	the science which studies illnesses and disease	____
4	chemistry	D	the science which studies energy, light, etc.	____
5	medicine	E	a place where experiments are carried out	____

F Choose the correct answer.

1 The study looked into the __*A*__ of young people towards science.
A attitude **B** mood **C** emotion
2 The most obvious ______ in the data is a gradual increase over time.
A fashion **B** motion **C** trend
3 A ______ 2% of people were able to name a scientist working today.
A just **B** mere **C** minor
4 The ages of the participants ______ from 16 to 29.
A covered **B** included **C** ranged
5 Ten per cent of the people asked preferred not to ______ a preference.
A tell **B** state **C** utter
6 Science subjects were most popular with people in the 18–24 age ______ .
A group **B** circle **C** set

Vocabulary boost: word formation

G **Write the correct form of the word in bold in each gap.**

PHYSICS

1 Most _physicists_ agree that the universe started with a Big Bang.
2 It's ____________ impossible to travel faster than the speed of light.
3 It's amazing to think that we can work out the ____________ laws behind nature.

CHEMISTRY

1 Although I studied chemistry at university, I never wanted to become a ____________ .
2 Silver and tin may look a little similar, but ____________ they're quite different.
3 Be careful when you are handling such dangerous ____________ .

BIOLOGY

1 There seems to be no ____________ reason why the animals are dying.
2 A number of ____________ think that life may have originated on another planet.
3 Mice and rats are ____________ very similar.

SCIENCE

1 To believe in UFOs without any real evidence is completely ____________ .
2 Do you accept the ____________ proof that climate change is caused by humans?
3 Is it ____________ possible to travel backwards in time?

Vocabulary boost: sciences

H **Match each science to the correct definition.**

1	anatomy	A	the study of ancient societies through old objects	_1E_
2	anthropology	B	the study of rocks	______
3	archaeology	C	the study of the weather	______
4	geology	D	the study of animals	______
5	linguistics	E	the study of the human body	______
6	meteorology	F	the study of languages	______
7	psychology	G	the study of the mind	______
8	zoology	H	the study of human cultures	______

I **CD, 10 Listen to these extracts from lectures. Write the subject of the lecture.**

1 Speaker 1: _geology_
2 Speaker 2: ______________________
3 Speaker 3: ______________________
4 Speaker 4: ______________________
5 Speaker 5: ______________________
6 Speaker 6: ______________________

5

EXAM PRACTICE

Student's Book pages 64–65

Reading

Vocabulary from the Reading text on pages 64 and 65 of the Student's Book

A **Match each word or phrase to the correct definition.**

1 marine life (title)	**A**	animal with a soft body and a hard shell		1H
2 mollusc (paragraph 1)	**B**	kind of plant or animal		______
3 creature (paragraph 1)	**C**	large fish with sharp teeth		______
4 species (paragraph 3)	**D**	very small living thing		______
5 albatross (paragraph 4)	**E**	animal		______
6 microbe (paragraph 4)	**F**	group of fish swimming together		______
7 school (paragraph 6)	**G**	large seabird		______
8 shark (paragraph 7)	**H**	general term for all life in the sea		______

B **Write a word from the text in the correct form in each gap. The paragraph and first letter of the word are given to help you.**

1 A new **e**xpedition has begun to the South Pole. (paragraph 1)
2 The **c**__________ shows that there are more species than we thought. (paragraph 3)
3 The **c**__________ of the project makes sure that everyone works together. (paragraph 3)
4 We used a large **w**__________ to lift the container onto the ship. (paragraph 3)
5 The harbour was full of **v**__________ from countries all over the world. (paragraph 3)
6 They invented a very strange-looking **c**__________ for exploring the seabed. (paragraph 3)
7 Before fridges, people often kept food preserved in salt in **b**__________. (paragraph 4)
8 We have created a **d**__________ that contains all the results of our experiments. (paragraph 4)
9 A special **s**__________ detects any large groups of fish that come near it. (paragraph 6)
10 A fishing **f**__________ consists of a number of ships working together. (paragraph 7)

C **Write a word from below in the correct form in each gap.**

~~accessible~~ confined cruise plunge shallow shatter

1 Technology means that the Antarctic is much more accessible than it used to be.
2 As it passes over the waterfall, the water __________ over 500 feet.
3 We're hoping to take a __________ around the Mediterranean this summer.
4 As I swam nearer to the beach, the water became __________ enough for me to stand up.
5 The effects of global warming are not __________ to just one area.
6 I was walking across the frozen lake when I slipped and the ice __________.

6 THE MEDIA

Reading

Student's Book pages 68–69

Wordbank

Vocabulary from the Wordbank on page 69 of the Student's Book

A Write a word from below in the correct form in each gap.

bulletin candid harassment merge ~~press~~ update

1 The *press* have been accused of making the story up.
2 When the two media organisations ______ , 100 people lost their jobs.
3 The man was found guilty of ______ and ordered to stay away from Madonna.
4 Turn to page 4 for our amazingly ______ photos of Tom Cruise!
5 Later in the programme, we'll bring you a/an ______ on the situation in Paris.
6 The station broadcasts a five-minute news ______ every hour.

Other vocabulary

Other vocabulary from the Reading section on pages 68 and 69 of the Student's Book

B Choose the correct answer.

1 Everyone thought *A* that the newspaper must have made a mistake.
A initially **B** primarily **C** essentially
2 He has built up a reputation for ______ going after the truth behind a story.
A reluctantly **B** relentlessly **C** eternally
3 Her career as a celebrity ______ came to a shameful end.
A inevitably **B** uncertainly **C** unsurely
4 Who came up with the ______ of reality TV?
A concept **B** thought **C** image
5 I believe that even world-famous celebrities should be allowed some ______ .
A loneliness **B** secrecy **C** privacy
6 *Frasier* was a comedy that ______ from 1993 to 2004.
A played **B** ran **C** showed
7 The BBC was ______ in 1922.
A set **B** erected **C** established
8 People are afraid because a number of ______ crimes have appeared in the media.
A high-powered **B** high-profile **C** high-level
9 The car crashed while being ______ by paparazzi.
A tracked **B** imitated **C** pursued
10 The media have ______ to the situation through irresponsible reporting.
A contributed **B** worsened **C** deteriorated
11 I think this issue needs to be seen in a ______ context.
A longer **B** higher **C** wider
12 The court decided that the celebrity had been at ______ in the case.
A blame **B** fault **C** responsibility

Vocabulary boost: topic vocabulary

C **Match each word or phrase to the correct definition.**

1 comment	**A**	story that no other newspaper is covering		1G
2 exclusive	**B**	title above a news story		____
3 feature	**C**	document for the press with information to base a story on		____
4 headline	**D**	story about shocking behaviour		____
5 editorial	**E**	longer article of general interest in a newspaper		____
6 press release	**F**	statement giving a newspaper's opinion		____
7 scandal	**G**	statement to the press when asked about a story		____
8 tabloid	**H**	newspaper which covers celebrity stories instead of serious news		____

D **Write a word or phrase from Exercise C in the correct form in each gap.**

1 Don't miss our *exclusive* on the recent story involving the Prime Minister.
2 It's my job to go through the ____________ each morning to see if there are any good stories.
3 The ____________ the next day was 'MINISTER FOUND GUILTY'.
4 There's an interesting ____________ in today's paper on global warming.
5 In response to the question, the man said, 'No ____________.'
6 I can't stand reading the ____________. They're just full of gossip.
7 In the ____________, the newspaper demanded the resignation of the person responsible.
8 There was a huge ____________ when the press found out what the politician had done.

Vocabulary boost: word formation

E **Write a word from below in the correct form in each gap.**

correspond edit journal photograph present publish ~~report~~

1 someone whose job is to find out the facts of a news story: *reporter* or ____________
2 someone who takes pictures to illustrate a news story: ____________
3 someone who regularly appears on a TV programme and talks to the viewers: ____________
4 someone employed by a news organisation to report back from another country: ____________
5 someone who decides what stories a newspaper is going to cover each day: ____________
6 someone who owns a newspaper and is in overall charge of it: ____________

Listening

Student's Book page 70

Wordbank

Vocabulary from the Wordbank on page 70 of the Student's Book

A Rearrange the letters to make a word that fits in the gap.

1 I think the *broadcast* (**AOSTCDBRA**) media in this country need to be regulated.
2 NBC have just ___________ (**SEMSOODCMINI**) a major new comedy show.
3 One of the biggest ___________ (**ISESUS**) at the moment is the economy.
4 During ___________ (**EEALHRRASS**), we realised that the play was very political.
5 It's difficult to put this show into a ___________ (**ENRGE**), but I'd call it a comedy.
6 All the ___________ (**NSOERELPN**) working on the show did a very professional job.

Other vocabulary

Other vocabulary from the Listening section on page 70 of the Student's Book

B CD, 11 Listen and decide who is speaking.

actor commissioning editor director producer ~~scriptwriter~~

1 Speaker 1: *scriptwriter*
2 Speaker 2: ___________
3 Speaker 3: ___________
4 Speaker 4: ___________
5 Speaker 5: ___________

Vocabulary boost: topic vocabulary

C Match each word or phrase to the correct definition.

cartoon documentary drama series game show
~~reality show~~ sitcom soap opera talk show

1 *reality show*: This is a programme where ordinary people are put into an unusual situation. Often, one of them is voted off each week.
2 ___________: This is a comedy programme about characters in a funny situation.
3 ___________: This is a fictional programme about ordinary people. It is usually broadcast a few times a week and it doesn't have a definite end.
4 ___________: This is a programme on which celebrities are interviewed.
5 ___________: This is a programme with characters drawn by hand or on a computer, which is usually aimed at children.
6 ___________: This is a factual programme about real people and real events.
7 ___________: This is a serious fictional programme that runs for a limited time.
8 ___________: This is a programme on which ordinary people compete against each other to win prizes.

Vocabulary boost: phrasal verbs

D **Choose the correct word.**

1 I'm just watching the end of this programme while I wait for the news to come **on** / **off.**
2 As he investigated the case, he came **across** / **to** evidence that he knew would be a major embarrassment to the government.
3 They broadcast a story about 'spaghetti trees' on April Fool's Day and people all over the country were taken **up** / **in**.
4 Global Media is trying to take **off** / **over** one of its smaller rivals, but the shareholders have rejected their latest offer.
5 I was taken **out** / **aback** at the way the interviewer spoke to the politician.
6 The government have been looking into the broadcasting industry and have put **down** / **forward** some interesting suggestions.
7 The minister looked very uncomfortable when the interviewer brought **off** / **up** what had been happening in his personal life.
8 I know you're watching this programme, but do you mind if I turn **out** / **over** for a second to catch the end of the football match?

E **Write a phrasal verb from Exercise D in the correct form in each gap.**

1 The director *put forward* his ideas for the show but they were impractical because they would have been too expensive to film.
2 The interviewer was clearly __________________ when the celebrity told him that her private life was none of his business.
3 I saw a new item about a couple of fraudsters who have been __________________ old people__________________ all over the country.
4 I wish you would just decide which channel you're going to watch instead of __________________ all the time.
5 When I saw Ryan, I decided not to __________________ the recent stories in the newspaper about him.
6 While I was reading the paper, I __________________ an article that mentioned the place where I work.
7 Channel Eight has just __________________ two other channels and plans to completely change their schedules.
8 There's no point ringing Grandma now because her favourite soap opera __________________ ten minutes ago and she won't answer the phone.

Speaking

Student's Book page 71

Grammarbank: Using conditionals

Grammar Reference, Section 11, page 106 of the Student's Book

A **Change the form of the verb in brackets and add any necessary words to complete the sentences.**

1. If you press this button, it *changes* (**CHANGE**) the channel on the TV.
2. You ________________ (**RUIN**) your eyes if you stay up watching TV all night.
3. If people watched less TV, they ________________ (**DISCOVER**) that there are many more interesting things to do.
4. Matt ________________ (**WATCH**) a lot more TV if his parents didn't limit the amount of time he can watch.
5. If we ________________ (**NOT HAVE**) a TV, I wouldn't be able to talk to my friends about the cool shows we've seen.
6. I might watch TV more if they ________________ (**MAKE**) programmes aimed at people like me.
7. If you ________________ (**SPEND**) all evening watching TV, you could have finished your homework by now.
8. I don't think TV ________________ (**INVENT**) if radio hadn't been invented first.
9. Life would have been very different when I was a child if we________________ (**NOT HAVE**) a TV in our house.
10. If I worked in the media, I ________________ (**MAKE**) sure that children's programmes were more educational.

B **Rewrite each sentence, starting with the words given.**

1. I can't buy a new TV because I don't have enough money.
   If I *had enough money, I would be able to buy a new TV.*
2. Everyone who owns a TV in the UK has to buy a TV licence.
   If you ____ .
3. I knew about the fire because I read about it in the paper.
   If I hadn't ____ .
4. Children who have a TV in their bedroom might watch programmes for adults.
   If ____ .
5. Alice didn't know Johnny Depp was on the news so she didn't watch it.
   If ____ .
6. The media reported the story and the missing girl was found.
   If the media ____ .
7. The press got hold of the email and the scandal became public.
   The scandal ____ .
8. People don't trust the tabloids because they make stories up.
   If ____ .

Wordbank

Vocabulary from the Wordbank on page 71 of the Student's Book

C Write a word or phrase from below in each gap.

however in spite of on the one hand on the other hand whereas while

MORAL PANIC

A moral panic happens when the general public becomes afraid of something because of reports in the media. The media reports create the impression that a problem is getting worse, (**1**) *whereas/while* statistics often show that the extent of the problem hasn't changed, or even that the situation is improving.

(**2**) ________________ , the media have a responsibility to report the news. When a particularly shocking crime takes place, it is understandable that they devote a considerable amount of time to it. (**3**) ________________ , they also have a responsibility to present what is happening in society accurately.

This doesn't happen in a moral panic. Public interest in the subject means that the media cover similar cases, often (**4**) ________________ the fact that they would not normally report on the incidents. This makes society seem dangerous, (**5**) ________________ much people's own experience tells them that this type of crime is not particularly common.

(**6**) ________________ people would normally forget about an incident, the media keep reminding them of it.

Vocabulary boost: word patterns

D Write a word from below in each gap. You need to use some words more than once.

about as for from of on with

1 ban someone *from* something
2 be capable ______ something
3 suffer ______ something
4 forgive someone ______ something
5 confuse something ______ something else
6 congratulate someone ______ something
7 describe something ______ something
8 hear ______ something from someone

E Write the correct form of a phrase from Exercise D in each gap.

1 Are journalists really *capable of* looking at events in a fair, objective way?
2 I don't think you can really __________ this newspaper __________ a tabloid.
3 I think you're __________ honest journalism __________ gossip and scandal.
4 I __________ the death of the king __________ a friend of mine.
5 The media should be free and shouldn't be __________ reporting on the incident.
6 He said he would never __________ the media __________ the way they ruined his life.
7 The minister __________ the media __________ the sensitive way they had reported the story.
8 The papers reported that the film star was __________ a serious illness.

Writing

Student's Book pages 72–73

Grammarbank: Using causatives

Grammar Reference, Section 12, pages 106–107 of the Student's Book

A Choose the correct answer.

1 My view is that children these days __A__ for them too much.
A have their lives organised **B** have organised their lives
2 Parents should consider ______ on their internet connection.
A having put a parental lock **B** having a parental lock put
3 We are ______ at the start of next week and I can't wait.
A having installed satellite TV **B** having satellite TV installed
4 You should ______ your car for you if it keeps breaking down.
A have someone check **B** have checked by someone
5 I need to ______ my computer for me.
A get someone repair **B** get someone to repair
6 It's time we ______ stricter controls on the media.
A had the government impose **B** got the government impose

B Write a causative form in each gap using the verb and noun given.

1 Reporters usually __*have their work edited*__ (**edit** / **their work**) before it is published.
2 Many people ______________________ (**influence** / **their opinions**) by what they read.
3 In my opinion, parents should ______________________ (**do** / **children**) more exercise.
4 My view is that we need to ______________________ (**realise** / **parents**) the harm TV can do.
5 In most countries the media ______________________ (**impose** / **certain rules**) on them.
6 All editors should ______________________ (**check** / **the facts**) before publishing a damaging story.

C Rewrite each sentence using a causative form.

1 Someone usually services our car for us once a year.
We __*have/get our car serviced*__ once a year.
2 An advertising agency makes all our commercials for us.
We ______________________ by an advertising agency.
3 Outside companies make most of the BBC's programmes these days.
The BBC ______________________ by outside companies these days.
4 A newspaper is delivered to our door every morning.
We ______________________ to our door every morning.
5 Does someone check every story that appears in the paper each day?
Do you ______________________ each day?
6 Someone took candid photographs of the celebrity for the magazine.
The magazine ______________________ candid photographs of the celebrity.

Wordbank

Vocabulary from the Wordbank on page 72 of the Student's Book

D **Write a word from below in the correct form in each gap.**

~~alleviate~~ analyse compound confront resolve

1 The government has given money to the people who lost their jobs. That *alleviates* the problem temporarily, but it doesn't solve the underlying problem.
2 The government needs to __________ the media over its handling of the case and not just ignore the problem.
3 The fact that so much of the media is owned by very few people just __________ the problem of media bias and something should be done about it.
4 It should be clear to anyone who __________ the situation objectively that the media have done a good job in exposing corruption.
5 The only way we can finally __________ the problem of media harassment of celebrities is to introduce a new law.

Other vocabulary

Other vocabulary from the Writing section on pages 72 and 73 of the Student's Book

E **Choose the correct word.**

1 It doesn't seem **thoughtful** / **reasonable** to expect the media not to report stories that they know the public are interested in.
2 The media's inability to regulate themselves is the real **cause** / **effect** of a large number of complaints.
3 There are various laws that exist to protect the rights of the individual, and **consequently** / **subsequently** the media are careful about the claims they make.
4 The mistakes in the report were **caused** / **due** to poor journalism.
5 The number of TV channels has increased recently as a **result** / **reason** of the changes to the regulations.
6 The need to provide for their families places great **commands** / **demands** on people.

F **CD, 12 Listen and match each year to the correct statement.**

1 1941 *F*
2 1946 ______
3 1970 ______
4 1985 ______
5 1987 ______
6 1996 ______

A No major media company can buy another major media company.
B Stations are allowed to broadcast as many advertisements as they like.
C No media company can own a radio and television station in the same market.
D Stations are no longer required to present a balanced view.
E There is no limit on the number of radio stations a media company can own.
F No broadcaster is allowed to reach more than 35% of the population.

Vocabulary boost: word formation

G **Write the correct form of the word in bold in each gap.**

DIRECT

1 The *director* spends a long time discussing the script with the writer.
2 I'm concerned at the ___________ the current government is taking.
3 The connection isn't obvious, but the scandal led ___________ to a change in the law.

FORTUNE

1 The media have been very ___________ to avoid further rules being imposed on them.
2 ___________ , my application to work at the company was turned down.
3 The reporter said that the explosion was the result of an ___________ accident.

HARM

1 Do you think television has any ___________ effects on children?
2 In my view, TV is ___________ entertainment and does not affect children badly at all.
3 The news report said that all the people involved in the crash escaped ___________ .

PERSUADE

1 TV advertisers use all their powers of ___________ to get you to part with your money.
2 Although the argument seemed ___________ , I could see a number of points against it.
3 Due to the ___________ of the politician's speech, voters returned his party to power for another term.

Vocabulary boost: phrases

H **Write a verb from below in each gap. You need to use some verbs more than once.**

bear draw give make raise take

1 *give* your opinion
2 ___________ someone's attention to something
3 ___________ sense of something
4 ___________ something in mind
5 ___________ control of something
6 ___________ someone's point
7 ___________ a question

I **Write the correct form of a phrase from Exercise H in each gap.**

1 I *take* your *point* , but I'm afraid I still don't agree with you.
2 We shouldn't allow a few large businesses to ___________ the media.
3 I'd like to ___________ to what it says on page 117.
4 Everyone had the opportunity to ___________ before the decision was made.
5 One role of the media is to help us ___________ a very confusing, fast-changing world.
6 The scandal ___________ about the President's ability to show strong leadership.
7 When you are talking about the media, you need to ___________ the effect the internet has had.

6 EXAM PRACTICE

Student's Book pages 74–75

Reading

Vocabulary from the Reading text on pages 74 and 75 of the Student's Book

A Find words or phrases in the Reading text which have a similar meaning to those below. The paragraph is given to help you.

1. living in a place before other people (paragraph 1) *indigenous*
2. second (of two things being discussed) (paragraph 1) ______
3. accepted or used by most people (paragraph 2) ______
4. not accepted or used by most people (paragraph 2) ______
5. very famous (paragraph 3) ______
6. able to express ideas well (paragraph 8) ______
7. separate and different (paragraph 8) ______
8. quick (paragraph 9) ______

B Write a word from below in the correct form in each gap.

aborigine breed ~~certificate~~ handout outback perspective policy portrayal satellite stakeholder standard state

1. I didn't believe I'd passed the exam until I finally had the *certificate* in my hand.
2. My dad says that too many people in this country rely on government ______ instead of trying to find a job.
3. If you get lost in the Australian ______, it can be very dangerous and even life-threatening.
4. The ______ of Australia are still struggling to achieve equality.
5. The ______ are all the people who are affected by a situation or by a decision and whose opinions should be taken into account.
6. All ______ of dog are closely related and originally come from wolves.
7. The reporter asked the minister what his party's ______ was on immigration.
8. The USA consists of 50 ______ and has a population of around 300 million.
9. The programmes produced by the station are of a very high ______.
10. From a local ______, very few people in this area will benefit from the investment.
11. The signals are sent around the world by ______ almost instantly.
12. I'd like to complain about the ______ of the black community in your recent documentary.

C Match each word to the correct definition.

1. merit *C*
2. represent ______
3. appeal ______
4. distribute ______
5. stereotype ______

A express the opinions of a group
B provide to people over an area
C deserve, be worth something
D assume what someone is like based on their race, etc.
E be attractive

7 LANGUAGES

Reading

Student's Book pages 78–79

Wordbank

Vocabulary from the Wordbank on page 79 of the Student's Book

A Rearrange the letters to make a word that fits the gap.

1 I know all the words but I still can't work out the *meaning* (**NAGMENI**) of the sentence.
2 You __________ (**MORF**) the noun by adding *-ion* onto the verb.
3 I use my diary to __________ (**SEPERXS**) how I really feel about the day's events.
4 Could you __________ (**YENVOC**) my congratulations to the successful applicant?
5 The meeting was only a __________ (**LIPARAT**) success as not many people turned up.
6 Sports such as boxing are based on a/an __________ (**RETINNHE**) desire to be violent.

Other vocabulary

Other vocabulary from the Reading section on pages 78 and 79 of the Student's Book

B Write one word in each gap.

1 How can you learn a language *without* the aid of a teacher or book?
2 I quickly pulled my hand back __________ the doorknob when I realised it had just been painted.
3 There's a wide range __________ linguistics courses available.
4 I usually use this dictionary __________ my main source of reference.
5 They produce the sound __________ knocking two animal bones together.
6 Language relies __________ a shared understanding of meaning between speakers.
7 In English, the gerund is sometimes known __________ the *-ing* form.
8 As I rested my bag __________ the wall, I realised the book wasn't in it.

Vocabulary boost: languages

C Write the language formed from the place name.

Place	Language
(**1**) Arabia	*Arabic*
(**2**) China	__________
(**3**) England	__________
(**4**) France	__________
(**5**) Germany	__________
(**6**) Greece	__________
(**7**) Italy	__________
(**8**) Japan	__________
(**9**) Korea	__________

Place	Language
(**10**) Poland	__________
(**11**) Portugal	__________
(**12**) Russia	__________
(**13**) Spain	__________
(**14**) Sweden	__________
(**15**) Thailand	__________
(**16**) Turkey	__________
(**17**) Vietnam	__________

D **CD, 13 Write a word from below in each gap. You need to use some words more than once. Then listen and check your answers.**

Bengali Dutch Flemish French Gujarati Hindi Punjabi Urdu

Canada has two official languages: English and (**1**) ___French___ .
More than 24 languages are spoken in India, including English, (**2**) ____________ ,
(**3**) ____________ , ____________ , (**4**) ____________ and (**5**) ____________ .
The national language of Pakistan is (**6**) ____________ .
(**7**) ____________ is recognised as the official language in Pakistan. Six main regional languages, including (**8**) ____________ , are also spoken in Pakistan.
The official language of the Netherlands is (**9**) ____________ .
The forms of (**10**) ____________ spoken in Belgium are often referred to as (**11**) ____________ .

Vocabulary boost: verbs of communication

E **Write a word from below in the correct form in each gap. You need to use some words more than once.**

ask call say shout speak talk tell whisper

1. Adam ___speaks___ French fluently so get him to get the train tickets.
2. I was playing with my friends in the park when my mum ____________ me in to ____________ me that my grandfather had been taken to hospital.
3. I ____________ Lucy whether she wanted to come but she ____________ she couldn't.
4. I'll ____________ you on your mobile a bit later on.
5. A child of eight should be able to ____________ the time, shouldn't they?
6. If you ____________ me, that building's going to fall down soon.
7. No ____________ during the exam! If I hear anyone even ____________ , there'll be trouble!
8. It was so windy on the cliff we had to ____________ to each other to be heard.
9. How do you ____________ 'goodnight' in Japanese?
10. I couldn't ____________ what it was at first, but as it got closer I saw it was a rat.
11. Don't ____________ out the answers. Just put your hand up and wait for me to ____________ you what the answer is. Then you can ____________ me.
12. I was ____________ to our neighbours earlier, and apparently they're moving house soon.

Listening

Student's Book page 80

Wordbank

Vocabulary from the Wordbank on page 80 of the Student's Book

A Write a word from the Wordbank in each gap.

1 If you *point* something out, you mention it.
2 If you ___________ through a list, you start at the top and work down.
3 If you ___________ something out, you use your printer to make a copy of it.
4 If you ___________ things together, you combine them.
5 If you ___________ something off with something, you begin it in a certain way.
6 If you ___________ an idea across, you manage to convey it.

B Rewrite each sentence using the word in bold.

1 Combine all the envelopes into one large pile. **TOGETHER**
Put all the envelopes together in one large pile.
2 Let's begin the talk with a short introduction. **OFF**
____
3 I'd like to mention that this is only a suggestion. **OUT**
____
4 Quickly read the article and underline all the names of people. **THROUGH**
____
5 You have to communicate the idea to your children that no means no. **ACROSS**
____
6 I'll make copies of the handouts tonight using my printer. **OUT**
____

▸▸▸ *Other vocabulary*

Other vocabulary from the Listening section on page 80 of the Student's Book

C Write the correct form of the word in bold in each gap.

1 I've finished the main part of the essay but I've still got to write the *introduction* (**INTRODUCE**).
2 Please read this ________________ (**INFORM**) sheet carefully before assembling the product.
3 The ________________ (**WRITE**) transcript of a ________________ (**SPEAK**) conversation always looks strange because we often don't speak in full sentences.
4 A cube is a three-________________ (**DIMENSION**) object where all the sides are of equal length.
5 Tomorrow night, Tony Hill will be giving an interesting ________________ (**PRESENT**) on the history of ancient Persia.
6 During the ________________ (**DEMONSTRATE**), they showed us how to do mouth-to-mouth resuscitation.

Vocabulary boost: gestures

D 🎧 **CD, 14 Write a word from below in each gap. Then listen to a lecture on gestures and check your answers.**

~~nod~~ roll shake tut wag wave wink

GESTURES

Gestures around the world vary depending on culture. In Britain, a number of gestures are used regularly.

British people often (**1**) ___*nod*___ their head to signify confirmation or approval. Basically, this gesture means 'yes'. When people (**2**) ____________ their head, they are expressing the opposite: negation or disapproval. Basically, then, this gesture means 'no'. When people in Britain (**3**) ____________ – that is, they make a small audible click with the tongue – that is also a sign of disapproval. Another sign of disapproval, often used by parents to small children, is to (**4**) ____________ your finger. This involves a small sideways movement of the index finger several times. To (**5**) ____________ is to move the whole hand sideways several times. This is used for greetings and saying goodbye.

To (**6**) ____________ at someone – that is, to quickly close and then open one eye – usually indicates that the person doing it recognises a shared secret or shared information between them and the person they are doing it to. It's often considered a humorous, naughty or cheeky gesture, and is usually only used informally.

If you (**7**) ____________ your eyes, you rotate both eyes upwards for a short time. This can be used to express a number of negative emotions including boredom, disbelief, annoyance and impatience.

Vocabulary boost: phrases with 'word'

E **Choose the correct word.**

1 The theatre got into financial trouble from the word (**go**) / **start** and closed within a year.
2 What did I think of the film? Well, **in** / **with** a word, rubbish.
3 We're all human. In **other** / **more** words, we all make mistakes.
4 I didn't believe a/an **individual** / **single** word he told me.
5 They told me I was sacked, or words **to** / **with** that effect.
6 The politician accused the journalist of putting words into his **ear** / **mouth**.
7 Could you put **in** / **over** a good word for me when you see the boss tomorrow?
8 Spending the night alone in a dark cemetery would be **too** / **very** scary for words.

F **Write a verb from below in the correct form in each gap.**

fail give ~~keep~~ say take

1 I promised that I wouldn't tell anyone, and I'm going to ___*keep*___ my word.
2 I ____________ you my word that I wouldn't tell anyone, and I won't.
3 Don't ____________ my word for it; see for yourself!
4 Just ____________ the word, and I'll come over and help you.
5 Words ____________ me when I walked in and everyone shouted 'Surprise!'

Speaking

Student's Book page 81

Grammarbank: Tense revision 1 – Using simple tenses

A **Choose the correct answer.**

1 Actually, I __B__ a little Dutch.
A am understanding **B** do understand **C** have been understood

2 ______ to Australia but I'd love to go.
A I never went **B** I've never been **C** I hadn't gone

3 Who ______ that phrasal verbs are always informal?
A told you **B** did you tell **C** you told

4 She ______ yet where she's going to study.
A didn't decide **B** hasn't decided **C** doesn't decide

5 We've just ______ that the French exam is next Tuesday.
A been telling **B** told **C** been told

6 What ______ when you realised you'd made a mistake?
A did you **B** did you do **C** you did

7 I ______ a few grammatical mistakes, but at least they understood me.
A did make **B** was making **C** make

8 Sally ______ her lunch right now so she'll call you a bit later.
A has **B** is having **C** has had

9 If you ______ there, we'd never have found the right platform.
A weren't **B** hadn't been **C** aren't

10 Why ______ consider taking evening classes?
A you not **B** not to **C** don't you

B **If the word or phrase in bold is correct, put a tick on the line. If it is incorrect, rewrite it.**

1 Who here **they have** written the essay? __has__
2 We **did only just sit down** when the fire alarm went off. ______
3 Students **are given** extra time if they have dyslexia. ______
4 When **had they** their oral interview? ______
5 Grigori's **been** to his English class and won't be back for a couple of hours. ______
6 Everyone **is loving** your accent, don't they? ______
7 What **did Phil say** when you told him you'd lied to him? ______
8 Who told you what time **was it**? ______
9 It's the first time **I'm hearing** of that language. ______
10 It was the first time **I'd ever been** abroad on my own. ______

Wordbank

Vocabulary from the Wordbank on page 81 of the Student's Book

C **Complete each sentence so that it means the same as the first sentence.**

Basically, I want to study abroad.

1 To get *to the point*, I want to study abroad.
2 To cut ____________, I want to study abroad.
3 In a ____________, I want to study abroad.
4 The point ____________ I want to study abroad.

Vocabulary boost: metaphorical phrases

D **Choose the correct meaning for each of the words or phrases in italics.**

1 It took me quite a while to fully *digest* all the information.
A explain **B** understand (circled)
2 Janet says she's going to quit her job, but I find that very hard to *swallow*. She's threatened to quit several times before and done nothing about it.
A believe **B** support
3 The word 'anaesthesiologist' is a bit of a *mouthful*, isn't it?
A difficult thing to say **B** difficult thing to understand
4 Dave said he's going to beat me in the match tomorrow but I'll make him *eat his words*.
A regret he was rude **B** admit he was wrong
5 That joke Hardip told at dinner last night was *in very bad taste*.
A not funny **B** offensive
6 The boss noticed Mandy was late this morning but I'm sure she'll manage to *cook up* a good excuse – she always does.
A invent **B** write down
7 We spent the whole evening *chewing the fat* about the old days at university.
A having a serious argument **B** having a friendly conversation
8 I've got an idea for a website I'd like you to *chew over*; I'd really value your opinion.
A invest in **B** think about
9 We're going to *eat them alive* in the debate tomorrow night.
A argue strongly with them **B** easily beat them
10 Let me *chew on it* overnight before making a decision.
A consider it carefully **B** discuss it with someone

Student's Book pages 82–83

Writing

Grammarbank: Tense revision 2 – Using perfect tenses

A **Each of the words or phrases in bold contains a mistake. Rewrite them correctly.**

1 It was the first time **I ever attempt** to write a poem so it wasn't very successful.
I'd ever attempted

2 **I'm translating** this article all morning and I'm not even halfway through.
____

3 The Nobel Prize for Literature had **never won** by an Australian before.
____

4 The novel **has been existing** as a concept for several hundred years.
____

5 By the end of the year, more than 50,000 euros **will give out** to first-time playwrights.
____

6 How long **you wait** before the book came out?
____

7 Do you think you **will finished** the article by then?
____

B **Write each verb in the correct form. Use contractions where possible.**

1 How many times *have we been* (**we** / **go**) to see that musical so far?
2 ______________ (**I** / **sit**) here for the past half an hour and I haven't written a single word.
3 The textbook ______________ (**fully** / **revise**) to take changes in the exam into account.
4 By the end of today, ______________ (**I** / **write**) more than 5,000 words.
5 ______________ (**there** / **have**) ever been a more ridiculous plot for a story?
6 Is it the first time ______________ (**you** / **ever** / **have to**) give a speech in public?

C **Choose the correct word.**

1 I've been learning Mandarin Chinese **from** / **since** I was five years old.
2 I've been finding out about the ancient Sumerian language **for** / **since** the past month or so.
3 Have you **before** / **ever** wondered what the language of the first humans was like?
4 At that point I hadn't **still** / **yet** decided which language to choose.
5 I've never met a Scottish person **already** / **before**. Will I understand her accent?
6 I don't feel that I've done enough listening practice **already** / **yet**.
7 Have you finished writing the essay **already** / **yet**? That was very quick!
8 **By** / **To** the end of next week, we'll have been living here for a year.
9 I've done three IELTS practice exams so **far** / **long**.
10 Have you really **ever** / **never** had English lessons? That's amazing! Your English is so good!

Wordbank

Vocabulary from the Wordbank on page 82 of the Student's Book

D **Choose the correct word or words. Be careful! More than one word may be correct.**

1 The cost of English language textbooks is (**particularly**) / **largely** / **strikingly** high in Greece.
2 The number of students on science courses is **mainly** / **particularly** / **considerably** lower than the number on language courses.
3 Lessons in these three countries are **mainly** / **largely** / **strikingly** in after-school hours.
4 The number of dictionaries actually sold is **particularly** / **strikingly** / **noticeably** low compared to the expected sales figures.
5 People learning English are **largely** / **strikingly** / **considerably** doing so between the ages of eight and eighteen.
6 There are **noticeably** / **largely** / **considerably** fewer students doing online courses than classroom-based learning.

▸▸▸ Other vocabulary

Other vocabulary from the Writing section on pages 82 and 83 of the Student's Book

E **Write a sentence or short paragraph using the word in bold so that it means the same as the first sentence.**

98% of the population speak English but only 4.8% speak Maori.

1 (**although**) *Although 98% of the population speak English, only 4.8% speak Maori. / 98% of the population speak English, although only 4.8% speak Maori.*
2 (**however**) ______________________
3 (**contrast**) ______________________
4 (**hand**) ______________________
5 (**while**) ______________________
6 (**whereas**) ______________________

A minority of the population knows Maori and a minority knows New Zealand Sign Language.

7 (**similarly**) ______________________
8 (**equally**) ______________________
9 (**way**) ______________________
10 (**likewise**) ______________________

Vocabulary boost: topic vocabulary

F **The gaps in each pair of sentences can be filled with the same word. Write the word in each gap.**

1 The dog *barked* loudly as we approached.
'Attention!' *barked* the sergeant aggressively.
2 Your ___________ sorry now doesn't change what you've done.
There's an old ___________ where I come from: 'the sky is always bluer than the sea'.
3 My stereo's not working properly – there's no sound coming out of the left ___________ .
He's not a native ___________ , but he's practically fluent.
4 Don't ___________ in front of your mother!
Do you ___________ to tell the truth, the whole truth and nothing but the truth?
5 From the ___________ on her face, I think she was teasing you.
Do you know what the ___________ 'make do' means?
6 'Shut up!' doesn't have a subject or an object, but it's a/an ___________ , isn't it?
He was given a ten-year prison ___________ .
7 If you're tired, why don't you ___________ down for a while?
Don't ___________ to me! I know when you're not telling the truth!

G **Write a verb from below in the correct form in each gap.**

accept admit apologise confess deny
doubt ~~persuade~~ refuse regret suspect

1 I initially thought going on a cruise was a bad idea, but Shareen's *persuaded* me it's a good way to visit a number of different places.
2 I asked my neighbour to move his car because it was blocking mine but he ______________ !
3 I really ______________ not carrying on with German when I had the chance.
4 I'm not totally sure who did that graffiti, but I ______________ it was one of the Hadley twins.
5 Adrian Charleston finally ______________ to the crime after his fingerprints were found on the stolen property.
6 You can't ______________ that you were in the town centre this afternoon – I saw you!
7 I'll ______________ to them for losing my temper, but frankly I had every right to be annoyed.
8 I just don't ______________ your argument; it's illogical.
9 I do ______________ that I lied, but it was only a white lie.
10 I don't ______________ you had good reasons for doing what you did, but it was still wrong.

7 EXAM PRACTICE

Student's Book pages 84–85

Reading

Vocabulary from the Reading text on pages 84 and 85 of the Student's Book

A Write a verb from the text in the correct form to complete the definitions.

1 If something *emerges*, it starts to appear. (paragraph 1)
2 If you can ____________ something from something else, you can tell the difference between them. (paragraph 2)
3 If you ____________ in an activity, you do that activity. (paragraph 5)
4 If you ____________ something, you use, handle or control it. (paragraph 5)
5 If you ____________ about something, you suggest a theory about or explanation for it. (paragraph 7)
6 If you ____________ something, you say it. (paragraph 8)
7 If something ____________ with something else, the two things fit together or are connected. (paragraph 8)
8 If something ____________, it happens at a faster rate. (paragraph 10)
9 If you ____________ something, you leave it out. (paragraph 11)
10 If you ____________ something, you add it or put it in. (paragraph 11)

B Write a word from below to replace the words in italics.

articulation by-product discomfort interaction isolation
jaws milestone ~~sequence~~ spurt variation

1 Film scenes are rarely shot in *order*. *sequence*
2 There's a *difference* between the number of male and female students on this course. ____________
3 Reaching the age of 21 is a/an *important occasion* in many cultures. ____________
4 You'll probably experience some *feelings of being uncomfortable* for the next few days. ____________
5 Exhaust fumes are a *result* of the combustion of fuel in the car engine. ____________
6 Working on my own from home, I don't get much *contact* with other people. ____________
7 It's the *not being with others* that many old people who live on their own find difficult to handle. ____________
8 Her clear *verbal expression* of the situation gives the poem added emotion. ____________
9 The shark menacingly opened its *mouth* wide. ____________
10 His *sudden increase* in height happened when he was 15. ____________

C Complete the table. Use a dictionary to help you.

~~babbling~~ cooing coughing gesturing growling grunting murmuring
sighing snorting squealing sucking swallowing yelling

body actions which always involve noise	*babbling*
body actions which sometimes involve noise	
body actions which don't involve noise	

8 HISTORIES

Reading

Student's Book pages 88–89

Wordbank

Vocabulary from the Wordbank on page 89 of the Student's Book

A **Rearrange the letters to make a word that fits the gap.**

1 I think that reading personal ___*accounts*___ (**OTSUCNCA**) of famous events really brings history to life.
2 Although it's important to take into account what ______________ (**EIEESSSTNWEY**) say, you have to remember that they're not always totally reliable.
3 Nobody knows the ______________ (**ECPISRE**) date for the invention of the wheel, but it was probably about 3500 BC.
4 Their book is based on ______________ (**NSEITEEVX**) research into the Industrial Revolution.
5 There is a ______________ (**GEEDNL**) which says that a city called Atlantis exists under the sea.
6 During the fifteenth century, there was a huge ______________ (**ITHFS**) in European culture that we refer to as the Renaissance.

▸▸▸ *Other vocabulary*

Other vocabulary from the Reading section on pages 88 and 89 of the Student's Book

B **Choose the correct word or phrase.**

1 It's hard to imagine that everything around us will (**eventually**) / **lately** disappear and be replaced by something else.
2 We don't know whether ancient statues really **resemble** / **copy** the people they were based on or whether they present an idealised image of them.
3 According to **ancients** / **historians**, the Silk Route was a key connection between the East and the West.
4 In order to get at the truth behind a historical event, you need to use a range of different **ways** / **techniques**.
5 Some of the portraits found on ancient Egyptian graves have a **greatly** / **distinctly** modern look.
6 There are some really interesting old **stone** / **rock** houses in this area.
7 It was a key development in human history when we started to use **tools** / **devices** to cut things and to hunt.
8 I expect early humans used sticks and rocks as simple **weapons** / **attacks** when they were fighting.
9 The Incas of South America had a **relevantly** / **relatively** advanced civilization.
10 Wood was no good for cutting because you couldn't give it an **edge** / **ending**.
11 Steel is **an alloy** / **a recipe** consisting of iron and carbon.
12 **Bronze** / **Silver** is made by mixing copper with another metal, tin, and is used in the medal you get for coming third in the Olympics.

C **Write a word from below in each gap.**

deliberate enormous fanciful junior ~~original~~
previous profound sharp vast

1 Although the book was based on an earlier work, the writer made a number of changes to the *original* story.
2 Nobody believes his ____________ theories that modern humans first appeared in Europe.
3 The discovery of fire must have had a/an ____________ effect on human societies of the time.
4 There is a/an ____________ difference between us and the ancient Greeks.
5 I first became interested in history when I was at ____________ school and we learned about ancient India.
6 This article seems to be a/an ____________ attempt to create fear in people's minds.
7 Be careful with that knife! It's really ____________ .
8 As you will no doubt remember from the ____________ lecture, most experts accept that modern humans appeared around 200,000 years ago.
9 The development of farming was a/an ____________ advance in human history.

Vocabulary boost: word formation

D **Write the correct form of the word in bold in each gap.**

ABLE
1 Dr Fernandez has the remarkable *ability* to make everything interesting.
2 Throughout history, people with a physical ____________ have faced fear, misunderstanding and prejudice from other people.
3 He was ____________ to give the lecture today for personal reasons.

EDUCATE
1 Don't you think that history should be a part of everyone's ____________ ?
2 I believe that ____________ have a duty to make sure that what their students learn in class is factually accurate.
3 Even though this video game is set in fifth century China, I really don't see that it has any ____________ value at all.

EXPERT
1 He was reluctant to give me a firm answer to my question because it wasn't his area of ____________ .
2 I watched as the archaeologist ____________ removed the delicate pot from the ground.

EXPLAIN
1 Many things about the building of the pyramids remain ____________ .
2 For some ____________ reason, he suddenly changed his mind!

HISTORY
1 Working through the ____________ records was the only way to find what I wanted.
2 I'd like to thank you all for being here on this ____________ occasion.

Listening

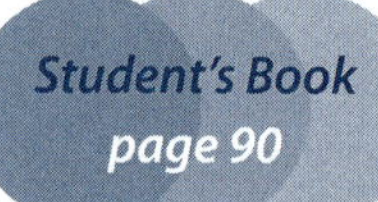

Wordbank

Vocabulary from the Wordbank on page 90 of the Student's Book

A **Write a word from below in the correct form in each gap.**

take ~~trace~~

1 The history of the town has *been traced* back to the year 1340.
2 Hearing that song again ________________ me back to when we first met.

time moment

3 At the ________________ , we were living in rented accommodation.
4 At the ________________ , we're living in rented accommodation.

about ready

5 Tina's a bit nervous at the moment, as she's ________________ to start a new job.
6 Are you ________________ to leave yet?

recall remind

7 This ________________ me of the time we got stuck in the lift. Do you remember?
8 As you'll ________________ , two of King Henry VIII's six wives were executed.

bound definite

9 There's ________________ to be a lot of traffic on the roads this evening.
10 Is there a ________________ connection between being left-handed and high intelligence?

lead make

11 The detour ________________ us to discover a beautiful little fishing village.
12 Even though we were on the guest list, we ________________ to wait in line with everyone else.

▸▸▸ *Other vocabulary*

Other vocabulary from the Listening section on page 90 of the Student's Book

B **Write one word in each gap. If no word is necessary, put a dash (–).**

1 My grandmother died *of* old age when she was 103 years old.
2 He actually worked ______ a waiter for a while before he became famous.
3 It was only after she'd gone ______ university that she decided to be a writer.
4 Why do more men than women commit ______ crimes?
5 Sumerian is considered ______ be the most ancient written language we know about.

6 Experts disagree ______ the age of the stones.
7 The film is based ______ a true story.
8 Bad historians criticise ______ the actions of people in the past; good historians try to understand them.

Vocabulary boost: remembering

C **Write a verb from below in each gap. If more than one verb is correct, write all the options.**

bring commemorate jog keep ~~learn~~ memorise
recall recollect remind reminisce

1 I want you all to ___*learn*___ this poem by heart this evening.
2 Actors have to ________________ large amounts of text very quickly.
3 The statue was erected to ________________ those who fought and died in the war.
4 Will you ________________ me in mind if any suitable jobs come up in the future?
5 It's lovely just to sit here and ________________ about the good old days.
6 You don't remember me, do you? Maybe it will ________________ your memory if I tell you where we met.
7 I know his name, but I just can't ________________ it to mind right now.
8 I wish I could ________________ what her name is.
9 Can I ________________ you all that your essays are due next Monday?
10 Can you ________________ anything at all about the accident?

D **Write a word from below in each gap to complete the definitions.**

memory memento memorial nostalgia reminder ~~souvenir~~

1 ___*souvenir*___ : something you buy or get on holiday or at a special event to help you remember being there
2 ____________ : something that helps you remember the past, or remember to do something
3 ____________ : looking back on the past with happiness
4 ____________ : something built to remind people of a person or event
5 ____________ : the ability to remember
6 ____________ : something you keep to remind you of a person or experience

E **CD, 15 Listen to six people talking. Match each person with what they are talking about.**

1 Speaker 1 ___*D*___
2 Speaker 2 ______
3 Speaker 3 ______
4 Speaker 4 ______
5 Speaker 5 ______
6 Speaker 6 ______

A nostalgia
B memory
C a memorial
D a reminder
E a souvenir
F a memento

Speaking

Student's Book page 91

Grammarbank: Tense revision 3 – Using continuous tenses

A **If a verb in bold is correct, put a tick. If it is incorrect, rewrite it.**

1 What **do you do** for the summer holidays this year? *are you doing*
2 You'**ve been practising** for hours now and it's time you had a break. ____________
3 I **go** out this evening with friends and we're thinking of going to the cinema. ____________
4 Before I started learning English, I **have learned** French for a year. ____________
5 I'm having an exam on Monday morning, which is why I'**ve been revising** for the last two days. ____________
6 My cousin **gets** married in Australia this weekend, so we are all travelling to Sydney to be there. ____________
7 I've got ten months of my course left so this time next year I **will work** in my father's company. ____________
8 By the end of this year, I **will learn** the piano for over nine years. ____________

B **Write the verbs in the correct form in each gap. If there is more than one correct answer, write all the possible answers.**

1 At the moment at school, we *are learning* (**LEARN**) about the history of Africa up to the start of the twentieth century.
2 I ____________ (**WORK**) hard all week so I ____________ (**LOOK**) forward to going away for a couple of days this weekend.
3 The economic situation seems ____________ (**GET**) worse at the moment and the government isn't doing enough to help ordinary people.
4 My brother ____________ (**STUDY**) history at university in Mexico now, but I ____________ (**HOPE**) to do medicine.
5 I ____________ (**GO**) on holiday next week and I ____________ (**PLAN**) to visit Rome.
6 At the time I was born, my parents ____________ (**LIVE**) in America temporarily.
7 I ____________ (**LEARN**) English for about six years now, and I ____________ (**HAVE**) private lessons for the last two.
8 By the time I fell asleep, I ____________ (**REVISE**) for over five hours.
9 They haven't finished yet, but it looks like a new road ____________ (**BUILD**) around the town.
10 Before we moved to this city, we ____________ (**LIVE**) abroad for three years.

C **CD, 16 Listen to this IELTS candidate and write a word or short phrase in each gap.**

1 She has been studying English for *seven* years.
2 She is currently having ____________ lessons as well.
3 As well as the language, she has been learning about the ____________.
4 She is planning to study ____________ at university.

Wordbank

Vocabulary from the Wordbank on page 91 of the Student's Book

D **Write one word in each gap.**

1 History isn't terribly important at school. Let me explain ___*what*___ I mean. It should be important, but I don't think it's emphasised enough in our educational system.
2 History is a bit of a waste of time because the world has changed so much that we can't learn anything useful from it. I'd also ____________ to add that it's often presented in a very boring way.
3 People don't think about history enough. What I'm ____________ to say is, people learn about history at school and then completely forget about it when they're older.
4 My country has had a very difficult history and we've had a number of natural disasters. If I ____________ just give you an example. We had a really bad earthquake a few years ago.

Other vocabulary

Other vocabulary from the Speaking section on page 91 of the Student's Book

E **Choose the correct word.**

1 I've always **admired** / **overlooked** my father for the way he has worked hard to keep a family.
2 The Roman Emperor **ruled** / **managed** over a vast empire that covered most of Europe.
3 There were **complaints** / **protests** outside the United Nations building involving thousands of people.
4 If the leaders had acted differently, then perhaps war could have been **escaped** / **avoided**.

Vocabulary boost: phrases

F **Write a word from below in the correct form in each gap. You need to use some words more than once.**

do fail make pass set take

1 The night before I'm about to ___*take*___ an exam, I always get very nervous.
2 The first time I got a low mark and ____________ an exam was a very depressing experience.
3 History was never a strong subject of mine, but I finally ____________ the exam at the second attempt.
4 I believe that you should ____________ advantage of all the opportunities that life offers.
5 Each of us has a responsibility to ____________ an example for the next generation.
6 It ____________ a long time to really gain an understanding of history.
7 Getting away from your books and getting some fresh air might ____________ you good.
8 I know he lost your book, but I'm sure he didn't ____________ it on purpose.

Writing

Student's Book pages 92–93

Grammarbank: Making complex sentences

Grammar Reference, Section 13, page 107 of the Student'sBook

A Rewrite each sentence starting with the word given.

1 If the diary was proved to be genuine, it would change history forever.
Were *the diary proved to be genuine, it would change history forever.*
2 If you went to Russia, which cities would you like to visit?
Were ____?
3 If the last Ice Age had not ended when it did, our civilization might well not have developed.
Had ____.
4 If the Romans hadn't invaded Britain, Hadrian's Wall would never have been built.
Had ____.

B Write the words in bold in the correct form.

1 Not only *did the fire damage* (**the fire** / **damage**) the building but it also destroyed all the books inside.
2 Under no circumstances ______________________ (**children** / **allow**) out alone in those days.
3 No sooner ______________________(**the war** / **end**) than a violent earthquake hit the country.
4 Neither ______________________ (**they** / **have**) the vote back then, nor ______________________ (**they** / **be**) able to enter public life.
5 Hardly ______________________ (**he** / **become**) Prime Minister when he had to resign due to ill health.
6 Not until 1969 ______________________ (**a human** / **walk**) on the Moon for the first time.
7 Rarely ______________________ (**there** / **be**) a more peaceful civilization since the Minoans.
8 Never ______________________ (**they** / **see**) Europeans before.

C Write one word in each gap.

1 There are more people on Earth today *than* there ___________ have been before.
2 There was so ___________ smoke ___________ they were unable to find the exit.
3 The news spread to ___________ an extent that, within an hour, half the country had heard it.
4 The flood-waters were so high that ___________ the church on the top of the hill was in danger.
5 The plan was ___________ complicated than we had anticipated it would be.

D **Write one word in each gap.**

Archimedes, (**1**) ___*who*___ was born in Syracuse in about 287 BC, is considered to be one of the greatest scientists and mathematicians (**2**) ____________ all time. Archimedes invented numerous mechanical machines, including the screw pump, (**3**) ____________ is named after him as the Archimedes Screw. One of the most famous stories about Archimedes concerns his discovery, (**4**) ____________ in the bath, of how to measure the volume and density of an irregular-shaped object. On (**5**) ____________ his discovery, Archimedes is believed to have shouted 'Eureka!', (**6**) ____________ is Greek for 'I've found it!'. (**7**) ____________ to put on his clothes because of his excitement, he then ran naked down the street. Archimedes died in approximately 212 BC (**8**) ____________ the Siege of Syracuse, (**9**) ____________ he was killed by one of the Roman soldiers who had just invaded the town and to (**10**) ____________ Archimedes had been disrespectful.

Wordbank

Vocabulary from the Wordbank on page 92 of the Student's Book

E **Complete the table. Include negative forms.**

Noun	Verb	Adjective	Adverb	Phrases
belief ________ ________	believe ________	________ ________	________	look/stare, etc. in ________ contrary to popular ________
doubt ________	________	________	________	________ Thomas
evidence	–	________ self-________	________	–

▸▸▸ Other vocabulary

Other vocabulary from the Writing section on pages 92 and 93 of the Student's Book

F **Choose the correct words or phrases. Be careful! More than one option might be correct.**

1. **Contrary** / **Contrary to** / **Against** popular belief, slaves were not used to build the Pyramids of Egypt.
2. There is some evidence to suggest this. **Although** / **However** / **Nevertheless**, none of it is conclusive.
3. **While** / **Although** / **However** the quote 'Let them eat cake' is often attributed to Marie Antoinette, there is no evidence at all that she actually said it.
4. This is, **in my opinion** / **in my view** / **according to me**, the most likely explanation.
5. **In scientists' view** / **In the opinion of scientists** / **According to scientists**, this is the most likely explanation.
6. One view that has been put **ahead** / **forward** / **up** by some academics is that the king actually escaped in disguise.

Vocabulary boost: irregular verbs

G Complete the table.

Bare infinitive	Past simple	Past participle
be	*was/were*	*been*
become		
begin		
break		
bring		
build		
buy		
catch		
choose		
come		
cost		
deal		
do		
drive		
eat		
fight		
find		
forget		
get		
give		
go		
have		
hear		
hold		
keep		

Bare infinitive	Past simple	Past participle
know		
lead		
leave		
lose		
make		
put		
read		
say		
see		
sell		
send		
set		
show		
speak		
spend		
spread		
stand		
steal		
take		
teach		
tell		
think		
understand		
win		
write		

8

EXAM PRACTICE

Student's Book pages 94–95

Reading

Vocabulary from the Reading text on pages 94 and 95 of the Student's Book

A Find words or phrases in the Reading text which have a similar meaning to those below.

1 the gas produced when water boils (paragraph 1) *steam*
2 a device for removing gas or liquid from somewhere (paragraph 1) ____________
3 places underground where people dig for coal, gold, etc. (paragraph 1) ____________
4 the outside area of an object (paragraph 1) ____________
5 long tube for carrying gas or liquid (paragraph 1) ____________
6 completely empty space, without air (paragraph 1) ____________
7 short stop before continuing again (paragraph 3) ____________
8 something which is burned to provide energy (paragraph 3) ____________
9 tools designed to hit other objects hard (paragraph 5) ____________
10 means of transport such as cars, buses, etc. (paragraph 7) ____________

B Write a word from below in each gap.

circular conventional dominant located
~~military~~ partial refined sophisticated

1 Many scientists during World War II were unhappy about the *military* use of their research.
2 No country can hold a ____________ place in the world forever. Another powerful country eventually appears to take its place.
3 Although I didn't get everything I wanted out of the meeting, I still considered it a ____________ victory.
4 Electric cars are much more efficient than ____________ cars.
5 Today's engines are very ____________ compared to the old, simple versions.
6 The man on the ground made a ____________ motion with his arms to tell the pilot to start his engines.
7 The capital city is ____________ in the south of the country, on one of the major rivers.
8 The design of the automobile was gradually ____________ over many years.

C Choose the correct word.

1 As we walked down the street, a small boy (**sprayed**) / **painted** us with water!
2 Are you sure the recipe says you have to **drop** / **chill** the soup to 5 degrees?
3 The window was so cold that my breath **condensed** / **melted** on it and I was able to write my name.
4 The machine is designed to **suck** / **blow** liquid up from the bottom of mines.
5 I didn't **set** / **go** out to become famous. It just happened!
6 I think we could help the environment by **altering** / **converting** the power of the sea into electricity.
7 We're going to have to speed **up** / **out** if we want to finish this before five o'clock.
8 Everyone has to learn to **adapt** / **change** to a world that is changing rapidly.

REVIEW UNITS 5–8

A **Choose the correct answer.**

1 I wish I had __________ more attention to my teachers at school.
A put **B** paid **C** had **D** sent

2 In our physics lesson, we __________ out an experiment with magnets.
A carried **B** brought **C** took **D** made

3 Kim's a liar – don't believe a __________ word she tells you.
A unique **B** separate **C** lone **D** single

4 Our manager pointed __________ a few problems with our suggestion.
A off **B** out **C** in **D** through

5 I thought what you said about the war was in very bad __________ .
A style **B** manners **C** sense **D** taste

6 Luck __________ a large role in our victory.
A did **B** became **C** produced **D** played

7 He promised to bear my ideas in __________ .
A head **B** brain **C** mind **D** thought

8 The police decided that nobody was at __________ in the accident.
A fault **B** blame **C** error **D** responsibility

8 marks

B **Write the correct form of the word in bold in each gap.**

FORENSIC SCIENCE

Forensic science is an important part of the modern-day war against crime. It often involves the careful collection of (**1**) __________ (**EVIDENT**) from the scene of a crime. If forensic scientists are (**2**) __________ (**FORTUNE**), they may find enough clues to be able to form a good (**3**) __________ (**EXPLAIN**) of what took place.

The forensic scientist interprets the clues, based on their (**4**) __________ (**EXPERT**) in a number of different areas. It takes real (**5**) __________ (**SCIENCE**) skill to bring all the clues together. They need to be (**6**) __________ (**KNOW**) about things as diverse as the marks a gun leaves on a bullet and the (**7**) __________ (**HARM**) effects of various chemicals. It involves separating the (**8**) __________ (**SIGNIFY**) details from irrelevant ones. A forensic scientist also needs to have the (**9**) __________ (**ABLE**) to bring everything together into a clear (**10**) __________ (**ARGUE**) that can then be used in court.

10 marks

C **Rewrite each sentence, starting with the words given.**

1 I had never seen such a shocking sight! Never ______________________________ .
2 Robert spoke to Alan for me. I got ______________________________ .
3 We didn't go to Moscow so we didn't see the festival. If we ______________________________ .
4 I only realised he was French when he spoke. Not until ______________________________ .
5 Emily said I should apply to university. Emily encouraged ______________________________ .

6 We could sign the contract tomorrow if they agreed. Were ______________________ .
7 Young people don't watch the news so they don't know what's going on. If young people ______________________ .
8 They are delivering our new sofa on Tuesday. We ______________________ .

8 marks

D Write one word in each gap.

1 My car broke __________ on the way to the meeting so I had to get a taxi.
2 I came __________ an old diary of mine while I was clearing my desk out.
3 The students put __________ some very interesting suggestions for the school library.
4 When we switched the lights __________ , the Christmas tree lit up the whole room.
5 I wasn't going to bring this __________ , but you owe me some money.
6 I wish you would make __________ your mind about what to wear!
7 Tim lost his job because the company he worked for was taken __________ by a rival.
8 Who do you think came __________ with the idea of sending text messages?

8 marks

E Choose the correct word or phrase.

1 I tend **thinking** / **to think** that we're going to lose the election.
2 If you **didn't go** / **hadn't gone** to university, then you wouldn't have got such a good job.
3 I **was coming** / **have been coming** to this restaurant for over ten years now.
4 Lisa seems to **be getting** / **have been getting** taller every time I see her!
5 If you don't mind **waiting** / **to wait**, the doctor can see you in half an hour.
6 I consider Sheryl **being** / **to be** one of my best friends.
7 At no point during the meeting **was anyone asked** / **did anyone ask** my opinion.
8 Why did you make Alison **go** / **to go** to the shop for you?

8 marks

F Write a word from below in each gap.

conventional deliberate essential partial
persuasive precise presentable profound

1 Losing his job had a __________ effect on him and it took him a long time to get over it.
2 Do you think alternative medicine can work in cases where __________ medicine has failed?
3 The operation was only a __________ success and he may need to have another one.
4 Make sure you look __________ before you go into the interview.
5 It seemed like an accident at first, but now I think it was __________ .
6 That point of view seems very __________ until you look at the actual facts.
7 Taking tough decisions is __________ to being a good politician.
8 Scientists have to take very __________ measurements during experiments.

8 marks

Total score: ______ / 50

KEY

Unit 1 THE ARTS

Reading Pages 2–3

Ex A
2 released **3** bring

Ex B
2 style **3** abstract **4** highlights/highlighted
5 animation

Ex C
2I **3**G **4**F **5**H **6**C **7**J **8**A **9**B **10**D

Ex D
2 specific **3** identifiable **4** animated
5 traditionally **6** originates/originated

Ex E
2 writer **3** singer **4** musician **5** actor/actress
6 painter **7** dancer **8** poet **9** creator
10 inventor

Ex F
2 spectator **3** listener **4** eyewitness
5 onlooker **6** audience

Ex G
2 documentary **3** play **4** performer **5** novel
6 instrument

Ex H
2 on **3** up **4** out **5** up **6** out

Listening Pages 4–5

Ex A
2A **3**A **4**C **5**C

Ex B
2 colourless **3** colourfully **4** confusion
5/6 confused/confusing **7** confusingly
8/9 critic/criticism **10/11** critical/uncritical
12 critically **13** dramatist **14** dramatic
15 dramatically **16/17** emotional/unemotional **18/19** emotionally/unemotionally **20** forgetful

Ex C
2 millennium **3** decade **4** quarter **5** century
6 season

Ex D
2 personalise **3** sympathise **4** advertise
5 familiarise **6** fantasised **7** economising
8 modernising

Ex E
2 performance **3** conceptual **4** pop

Speaking Pages 6–7

Ex A
2 I don't often get **3** We're rehearsing **4** Are you studying **5** does have **6** Do you know

Ex B
2 Have you already heard
3 The book has sold
4 I've ever seen
5 has she done
6 Lee's been worrying
7 Have you ever been
8 I've been trying

Ex C
2 since **3** just **4** still **5** ever **6** before
7 already **8** for

Ex D
2 TRUE **3** FALSE **4** FALSE **5** TRUE

Ex E
2 for **3** on **4** for **5** over

Ex F
2 many **3** a few **4** many **5** a few **6** lots

Ex G
2 but **3** because **4** such

Ex H
2 in having **3** to draw **4** of learning **5** to sell
6 in getting **7** to go **8** at remembering

Writing Pages 8–10

Ex A
From the data which <u>has presented</u> in this table, it <u>can see</u> that the cinema is becoming less popular with young people aged 14–18. Although the cinema <u>was mention</u> as a leisure activity by 68% of 14–18-year-olds ten years ago, today the figure is only 59%. In contrast, 70% of 19–23-year-olds <u>who questioned</u> said that they go to the cinema at least twice a month. In the next age group (24–37-year-olds), the cinema <u>was been chosen</u> by 65% of those asked.
2 can be seen
3 was mentioned
4 who were questioned
5 was chosen

Ex B
2 Over 1,000 people were asked for their opinions.
3 The study was designed to discover attitudes towards forms of entertainment.
4 Concerts were described as 'very enjoyable' by almost half of the people surveyed.
5 This problem can be solved by encouraging more art education.

Ex C
2 is considered
3 were asked
4 were/had been shocked
5 is/was/has been described
6 is/was preferred
7 be organised
8 be attracted
9 were interviewed
10 be interested

Ex D
2A **3**B **4**A **5**A **6**B

Ex E
Accept the answers below and any answers which use synonyms of words in these answers correctly.
2 a sudden increase followed by a steady decline
3 a sharp drop followed by a sudden increase and then a gradual decrease
4 a steady fall followed by a sharp rise and then a sudden drop
5 a gradual increase followed by a sharp drop
6 a sudden drop followed by a steady rise

Ex F
2 a slight
3 slightly
4 considerable

Ex G
2F **3**E **4**B **5**D **6**A

Ex H
2 of **3** from **4** on **5** in **6** into

Exam Practice Page 11

Ex A
2 tracing **3** elements **4** era **5** numerous
6 Prior to **7** depictions **8** lacking
9 authenticity **10** alleged

Ex B
2 a little less than **3** at first **4** extremely
5 not completely **6** almost **7** mainly

Ex C
2 patent **3** co-found **4** brand **5** models
6 mark **7** invisible **8** entire

Ex D
2 popularity **3** existence **4** uncertainty
5 performance **6** majority **7** developments
8 contributions

Unit 2 SOCIETIES

Reading Pages 12–13

Ex A
Phrase as used in reading section given first, other possibilities in brackets
2D **3**B **4**A **5**C (A) (D) (F) **6**E

Ex B
2 developing countries
3 unemployment benefit
4 national insurance
5 human rights
6 health care

Ex C
2 funds **3** authorities **4** shipments **5** roots
6 citizens

Ex D
2 aid **3** ideal **4** trade **5** poverty
6 co-operation

Ex E
POLITICS 2 political **3** politically
ORGANISE 1 organiser(s) **2** disorganised
3 organisation
LEGAL 1 legalise **2** illegal **3** legally
ECONOMY 1 economic **2** Economists
3 economical
SOCIETY 1 social **2** antisocial/anti-social
3 socially

Ex F
2 get **3** bring **4** vote **5** join **6** turn
7 comes / is brought **8** do

Listening Pages 14–15

Ex A
2 volunteered **3** caters/catered **4** issue
5 rude **6** fit

Ex B
2B **3**B **4**B **5**A **6**C

Ex C
2C **3**A **4**D **5**B **6**E

Ex D
2 tribe **3** crowd **4** society **5** gangs **6** club

Ex E
2 make **3** make **4** show **5** take **6** do **7** take
8 get

Ex F
2 do … a favour
3 make friends with
4 take care of
5 take … into account
6 get into debt
7 made … a promise
8 took pity on

Speaking Pages 16–17

Ex A
2 had been living
3 were living / lived
4 was
5 met
6 had been living / had lived
7 started
8 missed

Ex B
2 Tim had left the party when I arrived. / When I arrived, Tim had left the party. / When I arrived at the party, Tim had left. / Tim had left when I arrived at the party.
3 When you rang me, I had been doing my homework for ten minutes. / I had been doing my homework for ten minutes when you rang me.
4 My parents had been living abroad for six months when I was born. / When I was born, my parents had been living abroad for six months.
5 Wendy and Miguel had known each other for a year when I met them. / When I met them, Wendy and Miguel had known each other for a year. / When I met Wendy and Miguel, they had known each other for a year. / They had known each other for a year when I met Wendy and Miguel.
6 Liza and I were talking about Dan when he came into the room. / When Dan came into the room, Liza and I were talking about him. / When he came into the room, Liza and I were talking about Dan.
7 I had been waiting for half an hour when Kyle finally arrived. / When Kyle finally arrived, I had been waiting half an hour.
8 I went to university while we were living in France. / While we were living in France, I went to university.

Ex C
2 opinion **3** point **4** think **5** personal **6** far

Ex D
2 disagrees **3** agrees **4** disagrees
5 disagrees **6** agrees

Ex E
2 excitement **3**/**4** unexciting/excited
5 leafy **6** residential **7**/**8** resident/residence

Ex F
2A **3**E **4**F **5**D **6**B

Writing Pages 18–20

Ex A
2 despite **3** fact **4** even **5** Although

Ex B
2B **3**A **4**C **5**A **6**C

Ex C
2 sent Karl to prison, (even) though he was under eighteen.
3 spite of the fact that he wore a disguise, the police caught him.
4 Jane stole a mobile phone, in spite of having / the fact that she had lots of money.
5 was stolen, although I locked it.
6 is (still) a major problem, even though it's dropping in this area.

Ex D
2 hold **3** reached **4** takes/take **5** come

Ex E
2 community **3** offenders **4** service
5 circumstances **6** inmates **7** tackle
8 convicted

Ex F
2E **3**A **4**D **5**C

Ex G
2 decent **3** minor **4** ineffective

Ex H
2 fraud **3** blackmail **4** vandalism **5** robbery
6 burglary **7** kidnapping **8** murder **9** theft
10 arson

Ex I
2 blackmailer **3** burglar **4** forger **5** fraudster
6 kidnapper **7** murderer **8** vandal **9** robber
10 thief

Ex J
2 of **3** of **4** for **5** with **6** for **7** of **8** to

Ex K
2 TRUE **3** FALSE

Exam Practice Page 21

Ex A
2 diners **3** individuals **4** draped **5** satisfies/satisfied **6** summoned **7** assume **8** gossip
9 nomadic **10** elaborate **11** wealthy
12 fragrant **13** elementary **14** primitive

Ex B
2 significance
3 ceremony
4 hospitality
5 obligation
6 rank
7 compliment
8 courses
9 wreath
10 goblet

Unit 3 FUTURES

Reading Pages 22–23

Ex A
2 granted **3** data **4** likely **5** concept **6** Given

Ex B
2E **3**F **4**B **5**D **6**A

Ex C
2 with **3** of **4** on **5** in **6** of

Ex D
2 to **3** to **4** to **5** about **6** of **7** to **8** of

Ex E
2 consensus **3** source **4** atom **5** encounter
6 objection **7** benefit

Ex F
2 practicalities **3** agreement **4** potentially
5 necessarily **6** reality **7** likelihood

Ex G
2 up **3** into **4** out **5** down **6** on

Listening Pages 24–25

Ex A
2 initially **3** reminded **4** estimates **5** current

Ex B
2 star **3** galaxy **4** Way **5** universe **6** System

Ex C
2 collide **3** collision **4** merge **5** agreement
6 close

Ex D
2 decision **3** conclusion **4** permission

5 invasion **6** admission (NB: 'admittance' also exists) **7** persuasion **8** exclusion **9** division **10** provision

Ex E

2 ✓ **3** divisible **4** permissible **5** ✓ **6** accessible **7** sensible **8** ✓ **9** possible **10** ✓ **11** horrible **12** responsible **13** ✓ **14** flexible **15** ✓

Ex F

2 (from) taking off **3** to become **4** of not knowing/having known **5** to seeing **6** to leave **7** seeing/having seen **8** of spending **9** (from) having

Speaking Pages 26–27

Ex A

3 will live/will be living/are going to live/are going to be living

4 ✓

5 I'm going to work/I'll work/I'm working I'm going to be working/I'll be working

6 ✓

7 We're not going (to go)/We aren't going (to go)/We won't be going

Ex B

2 I get/I've got **3** lands/has landed **4** you do/you're doing

Ex C

2 be **3** won't have **4** be living/working/etc.

Ex D

2 ✓ **3** will still be using **4** ✓ **5** ✓

6 it happens

Ex E

2 It's highly/very unlikely (that) it'll snow/to snow tomorrow.

3 It's impossible to know for sure, but maybe there is life after death!

4 Perhaps our grandchildren will be able to travel round the Solar System.

5 Do you think UFOs may be secret military planes?

6 It's/There's a possibility/One possibility is (that) what you saw was a satellite.

7 She's highly/very unlikely to fail the exam. It's highly/very unlikely (that) she'll fail the exam.

Ex F

2 of winning **3** they're going to offer **4** the **5** a **6** by **7** chances are **8** of

Ex G

2 in **3** wish **4** believe **5** out **6** With

Writing Pages 28–30

Ex A

2 produced **3** having examined **4** Having **5** Given **6** driving **7** Having seen **8** being stirred **9** Having been transferred

Ex B

2 Taken/Having been taken **3** entering **4** given off **5** checking/having checked **6** regulating **7** being placed **8** Having been washed **9** Having made

Ex C

2 After connecting the cables, an operator turns on the equipment.

3 Wearing a mask, a skilled technician spray-paints the wood.

4 Looking at the map, we/I/etc., saw/noticed/etc., (that) the town was six kilometres away.

5 Having been assembled, the furniture was/is put into position.

Ex D

2 as **3** of **4** like **5** of **6** into **7** of **8** in

Ex E

2 The process consists of a number of stages.

3 The box is the same height as a human.

4 The machine is larger than a car engine.

5 The skyscraper is shaped like an enormous cigar./The skyscraper is/has the shape of an enormous cigar.

6 The area is divided into four sections.

7 The wings are triangular in shape.

8 All the furniture is made of wood.

9 The control panel is the size of/same size as a small laptop.

10 The interior is more colourful than the exterior.

Ex F

2F **3**A **4**E **5**B **6**G **7**C

Ex G

2 After **3** Shortly **4** stage **5** where

Ex H

Adjective	Noun	Verb
long	length	elongate lengthen
short	shortness	shorten
high	height	heighten
low	lowness	lower
deep	depth	deepen
wide	width	widen
narrow	narrowness	narrow
large	largeness	enlarge

Ex I

Noun	Adjective
size	sizeable
space	spacious
spot	spotless
substance	substantial
extend	extensive
signify	significant
consider	considerable

Exam Practice Page 31

Ex A

2 foreseeing **3** predict **4** forecast **5** sensing

Ex B

2 medium **3** perception **4** déjà vu **5** Clairvoyance **6** gut **7** Instinct **8** premonition **9** hunch **10** paradox

Ex C

2 paranormal **3** psychic **4** mundane **5** compelling **6** bizarre **7** random **8** consistent **9** obsolete **10** poor

Unit 4 ENVIRONMENTS

Reading Pages 32–33

Ex A

2 speed **3** low **4** recycled **5** affordable **6** Waste **7** environmentally **8** carbon

Ex B

2 essential **3** rural **4** cost-effective **5** reliable **6** urban **7** efficient **8** suburban

Ex C

2 was fined **3** are adhered **4** is/was aimed **5** have been drawn up **6** aspire/aim **7** assume(d) **8** is anticipated/assumed

Ex D

2 out **3** down **4** away **5** out **6** off **7** up

Ex E

2 extinction **3** destruction **4** neighbourhood **5** lightning **6** surroundings **7** Industrial **8** harmless **9** residential **10** explanation

Listening Pages 34–35

Ex A

2 continental **3** lush **4** massive **5** monsoon **6** inhospitable

Ex B

2 skyscraper **3** nickname **4** dune **5** highlands **6** vegetation **7** per **8** northern

Ex C

2 10 cm

3 4.5/4½ m

4 7 m^2

5 21 g

6 2 kg

7 10 t
8 2.25/2¼ l
9 50 kph/km/h/kmph
10 18 °C

Ex D
2 100
3 1,000
4 1,000
5 m^2
6 m^3
7 0 °C
8 100 °C

Ex E
2 inches
3/4 feet/yards
5/6 pounds/stones
7/8 pints/gallons
9 tonnes
10 Fahrenheit

Ex F
2 12
3 3
4 91.44
5 1,760
6 1,609.344

Speaking Pages 36–37

Ex A

Always countable	Always singular uncountable
book fact job programme sheep suitcase	luggage advice furniture housework information knowledge money news

Always plural uncountable	Both countable and uncountable depending on meaning
clothes groceries jeans scissors trousers	time chocolate glass hair paper work

Ex B
2 Are **3** is **4** many

Ex C
2 – **3** the **4** – **5** the **6** a **7** the **8** the **9** The
10 – **11** the **12** – **13** a **14** – **15** an
16 – **17** the **18** the/– **19** The **20** –

Ex D
2 little – They didn't give me a lot of
3 few – Some
4 few – Not a lot of
5 little – They gave me some
6 Few – Not many

Ex E
2 than **3** didn't **4** prefer **5** rather **6** Would

Ex F
2 Would, rather **3** Would, didn't/did **4** not
5 Do **6** rather, had

Ex G
2 to bed **3** to work **4** for a swim **5** abroad
6 camping **7** sightseeing **8** on a tour **9** by train/bus **10** on foot

Writing Pages 38–40

Ex A
2 must **3** can't ... must **4** has **5** could **6** Do you need **7** couldn't

Ex B
2 have bought **3** have been **4** have been built **5** happen **6** have happened
7 to have ... look **8** have been arrested

Ex C
2 We must have made a mistake.
3 The council ought to renovate the old mill.
4 You shouldn't have bought a car that uses so much petrol.
5 If you have a solar-powered water heater, you don't need to use electricity to heat the water.

Ex D
2 Having ... that **3** In/By **4** the ... hand
5 Even **6** if **7** Despite **8** Although/Though/While

Ex E
Phrase as used in writing section given first, other possibilities in brackets
2F **3**A(D) **4**B **5**G(D) **6**E **7**D(C/F) **8**C(F)

Ex F
1 b taken
2 a happens **b** place
3 a result **b** reason
4 a same **b** Similarly/Likewise
5 a Nonetheless **b** Nevertheless

Ex G
2 approve, telling **3** permitted **4** deny
5 confessed **6** recognise **7** question
8 challenge **9** comprehend **10** trust, accept

Ex H

Verb	Noun
acknowledge	acknowledgement
agree	Positive: agreement Negative:disagreement
approve	Positive: approval Negative: disapproval
challenge	challenge
comprehend	Positive: comprehension Negative: incomprehension
confess	confession
deny	denial
dispute	dispute
permit	permission
recognise	recognition
trust	Positive: trust Negative: distrust/mistrust

Exam Practice Page 41

Ex A
2D **3**G **4**A **5**B **6**I **7**C **8**E **9**H

Ex B
2 not obvious but quiet and clever
3 rough and sharp **4** clear **5** rare **6** extreme
7 thoughtful **8** water **9** pleasant

Ex C
2 inspire **3** recede **4** rant **5** melt
6 collaborate **7** dismantle **8** donate **9** fund

Review Units 1–4 Pages 42–43

A
1B **2**A **3**B **4**D **5**C **6**A **7**D **8**D

B
1 musicians **2** unanswered **3** disagreement
4 accurately **5** confusion **6** originated
7 impossible **8** certainty **9** likelihood
10 natural

C
1 were given their exam results by Mrs Johnson.
2 been to Dubai since 2006.
3 of (my/me) setting my alarm clock, I didn't wake up on time./of the fact (that) I set…
4 as I'm concerned, the advantages far outweigh the disadvantages.
5 might/could/may be a storm later today./There is a possibility (that) there might/could/may/will be…
6 written the essay, she checked it carefully.
7 have been easy for you to organise the event on your own.

8 have taken the wrong turning back there.

D

1 out **2** down **3** on **4** on **5** in **6** up **7** up **8** out

E

1 of **2** of **3** to **4** in **5** on **6** to **7** on **8** with

F

1 fortnight **2** funds **3** opponent **4** nickname **5** famine **6** audience **7** valley **8** objection

Unit 5 SCIENCES

Reading Pages 44–45

Ex A

2 nuclear **3** originated **4** elements **5** calculated **6** orbits

Ex B

2 supernova **3** Solar System **4** exoplanet **5** position **6** brightness **7** mass **8** carbon **9** hydrogen **10** iron **11** helium

Ex C

2 expands **3** convert **4** demoted

Ex D

2 application **3** calculation **4** conversion **5** destruction **6** erosion **7** expansion **8** expectation **9** observation **10** production **11** recognition **12** solution

Ex E

2 accusation **3** recognition **4** erosion **5** expectation **6** destruction **7** application **8** solution

Ex F

2J **3**G **4**F **5**A **6**H **7**B **8**D **9**E **10**I

Listening Pages 46–47

Ex A

2 estimate **3** device **4** boot **5** elementary

Ex B

2 magnet **3** ball bearing **4** Tissue paper **5** needle **6** compass

Ex C

2 tissue paper **3** bowl **4** compass **5** ball bearings **6** magnet

Ex D

2 on **3** down **4** out **5** up **6** out

Ex E

2 carry out **3** broke down **4** came up with **5** switched on **6** find out

Ex F

2 in **3** of **4** of **5** from **6** on

Ex G

2 on **3** on **4** to **5** on **6** for

Ex H

2 was responsible for **3** depends on **4** apologised for **5** proud of **6** convince, of **7** object to **8** believe in **9** benefit from **10** rely on **11** comment on **12** approve of

Speaking Pages 48–49

Ex A

+ *-ing*	+ full infinitive
admit consider deny enjoy like mind risk suggest	afford choose fail hope intend like manage offer plan refuse tend wish

+ object + full infinitive	+ object + bare infinitive
allow cause encourage tell	let make suggest

Ex B

2 to pursue **3** to follow **4** to satisfy **5** applying **6** to succeed **7** to relax **8** to become/becoming **9** working **10** to do **11** to commit **12** to stick

Ex C

2 to check **3** asking **4** meeting **5** saying **6** quitting **7** to send **8** to ring

Ex D

2 well **3** worth **4** like **5** addition **6** further

Ex E

2 pay **3** have **4** take **5** give **6** make **7** make **8** play (have/take a role in a play in the theatre)

Ex F

2 made up your mind about **3** have an effect on **4** take, for granted **5** gave, the impression **6** made a mistake **7** take control of **8** play a role

Writing Pages 50–52

Ex A

2 why/that **3** which **4** where **5** which/that **6** whose **7** when/that **8** where

Ex B

2 it **3** ✓ **4** he **5** they **6** she

Ex C

2 Iron, whose chemical symbol is Fe, conducts electricity./Iron, which conducts electricity, has the chemical symbol Fe.
3 I saw a documentary which/that explained how magnets work.
4 Dr Carlisle, who was an expert in genetics, has died./Dr Carlisle, who has died, was an expert in genetics.
5 Hydrogen, which explodes easily, used to be used in airships./Hydrogen, which used to be used in airships, explodes easily.
6 I found an article which/that was all about working in science.

Ex D

2 noticeable **3** central **4** prominent **5** striking **6** essential

Ex E

2A **3**D **4**B **5**C

Ex F

2C **3**B **4**C **5**B **6**A

Ex G

PHYSICS 2 physically **3** physical **CHEMISTRY 1** chemist **2** chemically **3** chemicals **BIOLOGY 1** biological **2** biologists **3** biologically **SCIENCE 1** unscientific **2** scientific **3** scientifically

Ex H

2H **3**A **4**B **5**F **6**C **7**G **8**D

Ex I

2 archaeology **3** anthropology **4** anatomy **5** psychology **6** meteorology

Exam Practice Page 53

Ex A

2A **3** E **4** B **5** G **6** D **7** F **8** C

Ex B

2 census **3** coordinator **4** winch **5** vessels **6** contraption **7** barrels **8** database **9** sensor **10** fleet

Ex C

2 plunges **3** cruise **4** shallow **5** confined **6** shattered

Unit 6 THE MEDIA

Reading Pages 54–55

Ex A

2 merged **3** harassment **4** candid **5** update **6** bulletin/update

Ex B

2B **3**A **4**A **5**C **6**B **7**C **8**B **9**C **10**A **11**C **12**B

Ex C

2A **3**E **4**B **5**F **6**C **7**D **8**H

Ex D

2 press releases **3** headline **4** feature **5** comment **6** tabloids **7** editorial **8** scandal

Ex E

1 journalist
2 photographer
3 presenter
4 correspondent
5 editor
6 publisher

Listening Pages 56–57

Ex A
2 commissioned **3** issues **4** rehearsals **5** genre **6** personnel

Ex B
2 commissioning editor **3** director **4** actor **5** producer

Ex C
2 sitcom **3** soap opera **4** talk show **5** cartoon **6** documentary **7** drama series **8** game show

Ex D
2 across **3** in **4** over **5** aback **6** forward **7** up **8** over

Ex E
2 taken aback **3** taking, in **4** turning over **5** bring up **6** came across **7** taken over **8** came on

Speaking Pages 58–59

Ex A
2 will ruin **3** would/might/could discover **4** would/might/could watch **5** didn't have **6** made **7** hadn't spent **8** would have been invented **9** hadn't had **10** would make

Ex B
2 own a TV in the UK, you have to buy a TV licence.
3 read about the fire in the paper, I wouldn't have known about it./read about it in the paper, I wouldn't have known about the fire.
4 children have a TV in their bedroom, they might watch programmes for adults.
5 Alice had known Johnny Depp was on the news, she would have watched it.
6 hadn't reported the story, the missing girl wouldn't have been found.
7 wouldn't have become public if the press hadn't got hold of the email.
8 the tabloids didn't make stories up, people would trust them.

Ex C
2 On the one hand **3** On the other hand/ However **4** in spite of **5** however **6** While/ Whereas

Ex D
2 of **3** from **4** for **5** with **6** on **7** as **8** about

Ex E
2 describe ... as **3** confusing ... with **4** heard about ... from **5** banned from **6** forgive ... for **7** congratulated ... on **8** suffering from

Writing Pages 60–62

Ex A
2B **3**B **4**A **5**B **6**A

Ex B
2 have/get their opinions influenced
3 have their children do/get their children to do
4 have parents realise/get parents to realise
5 have/get certain rules imposed
6 have/get the facts checked/have someone check the facts/get someone to check the facts

Ex C
2 have/get all our commercials made
3 has/gets most of its programmes made
4 have/get a newspaper delivered
5 have/get every story checked/have someone check every story/get someone to check every story
6 had someone take/got someone to take

Ex D
2 confront **3** compounds **4** analyses **5** resolve

Ex E
2 cause **3** consequently **4** due **5** result **6** demands

Ex F
2A **3**C **4**B **5**D **6**E

Ex G
DIRECT 2 direction **3** indirectly **FORTUNE 1** fortunate **2** Unfortunately **3** unfortunate
HARM 1 harmful **2** harmless **3** unharmed
PERSUADE 1 persuasion **2** persuasive **3** persuasiveness

Ex H
2 draw **3** make **4** bear **5** take **6** take **7** raise

Ex I
2 take control of **3** draw your attention **4** give their/an opinion **5** make sense of **6** raised/raises a/the question **7** bear in mind

Exam Practice Page 63

Ex A
2 latter **3** mainstream **4** fringe **5** legendary **6** articulate **7** unique **8** rapid

Ex B
2 handouts **3** outback **4** aborigines **5** stakeholders **6** breeds **7** policy **8** states **9** standard **10** perspective **11** satellite **12** portrayal

Ex C
2A **3**E **4**B **5**D

Unit 7 LANGUAGES

Reading Pages 64–65

Ex A
2 form **3** express **4** convey **5** partial **6** inherent

Ex B
2 from **3** of **4** as **5** by **6** on **7** as **8** against

Ex C

Place	Language
China	Chinese
England	English
France	French
Germany	German
Greece	Greek
Italy	Italian
Japan	Japanese
Korea	Korean
Poland	Polish
Portugal	Portuguese
Russia	Russian
Spain	Spanish
Sweden	Swedish
Thailand	Thai
Turkey	Turkish
Vietnam	Vietnamese

Ex D
2/3/4/5 Hindi, Bengali, Gujarati, Punjabi, Urdu (in any order) **6** Urdu **7** English **8** Punjabi **9** Dutch **10** Dutch **11** Flemish

Ex E
2 called ... tell **3** asked ... said **4** call **5** tell **6** ask **7** talking/speaking ... whisper/ whispering **8** shout **9** say **10** tell/say **11** shout ... ask / tell **12** talking/speaking

Listening Pages 66–67

Ex A
2 go (read/work) **3** print **4** put **5** start **6** get (put)

Ex B
2 Let's start off the talk/start the talk off with a short introduction.
3 I'd like to point out that this is only a suggestion.
4 Quickly read/go through the article and underline all the names of people.
5 You have to get across the idea/get the idea across to your children that no means no.
6 I'll print out copies of the handouts tonight (using my printer)./I'll print copies of the handouts out tonight (using my printer).

Ex C
2 information **3** written, spoken **4** dimensional **5** presentation **6** demonstration

Ex D
2 shake **3** tut **4** wag **5** wave **6** wink **7** roll

Ex E
2 in **3** other **4** single **5** to **6** mouth **7** in

8 too

Ex F

2 gave **3** take **4** say **5** failed

Speaking Pages 68–69

Ex A

2B **3**A **4**B **5**C **6**B **7**A **8**B **9**B **10**C

Ex B

2 had only just sat down **3** ✓ **4** did/do they have **5** gone **6** loves **7** ✓ **8** it was **9** I've heard **10** ✓

Ex C

2 a long story short **3** nutshell **4** is (that)

Ex D

2A **3**A **4**B **5**B **6**A **7**B **8**B **9**B **10**A

Writing Pages 70–72

Ex A

2 I've been translating
3 never been won
4 has existed
5 will have been given out
6 had you been waiting
7 will have finished

Ex B

2 I've been sitting
3 has/had been fully/was fully revised
4 I'll have written
5 Has/Had there
6 you've ever had to

Ex C

2 for **3** ever **4** yet **5** before **6** yet **7** already **8** By **9** far **10** never

Ex D

2 considerably **3** mainly/largely **4** particularly/strikingly/noticeably
5 largely **6** noticeably/considerably

Ex E

2 98% of the population speak English. However, only 4.8% speak Maori.
3 98% of the population speak English. In contrast, only 4.8% speak Maori.
4 98% of the population speak English. On the other hand, only 4.8% speak Maori.
5 While 98% of the population speak English, only 4.8% speak Maori./98% of the population speak English, while only 4.8% speak Maori.
6 Whereas 98% of the population speak English, only 4.8% speak Maori./98% of the population speak English, whereas only 4.8% speak Maori.
7 A minority of the population knows Maori. Similarly, a minority knows New Zealand Sign Language.
8 A minority of the population knows Maori. Equally, a minority knows New Zealand Sign Language.
9 A minority of the population knows Maori. In the same/a similar way, a minority knows New Zealand Sign Language.
10 A minority of the population knows Maori. Likewise, a minority knows New Zealand Sign Language.

Ex F

2 saying **3** speaker **4** swear **5** expression
6 sentence **7** lie

Ex G

2 refused **3** regret **4** suspect **5** confessed
6 deny **7** apologise **8** accept **9** admit/accept **10** doubt/deny

Exam Practice Page 73

Ex A

2 distinguish **3** engage **4** manipulate
5 hypothesise **6** utter **7** correlates
8 accelerates **9** omit **10** insert

Ex B

2 variation **3** milestone **4** discomfort
5 by-product **6** interaction **7** isolation
8 articulation **9** jaws **10** spurt

Ex C

body actions which always involve noise	babbling cooing coughing growling grunting murmuring sighing snorting squealing yelling
body actions which sometimes involve noise	sucking swallowing
body actions which don't involve noise	gesturing

Unit 8 HISTORIES

Reading Pages 74–75

Ex A

2 eyewitnesses **3** precise **4** extensive
5 legend **6** shift

Ex B

2 resemble **3** historians **4** techniques
5 distinctly **6** stone **7** tools **8** weapons
9 relatively **10** edge **11** an alloy **12** Bronze

Ex C

2 fanciful **3** profound/enormous **4** vast/enormous/profound **5** junior **6** deliberate
7 sharp **8** previous **9** enormous

Ex D

ABLE 2 disability **3** unable **EDUCATE**
1 education **2** educators **3** educational
EXPERT 1 expertise **2** expertly **EXPLAIN**
1 unexplained **2** inexplicable **HISTORY**
1 historical **2** historic

Listening Pages 76–77

Ex A

2 takes/took **3** time **4** moment **5** about
6 ready **7** reminds **8** recall **9** bound
10 definite **11** led **12** were made

Ex B

2 as **3** to **4** – **5** to **6** about/on **7** on **8** –

Ex C

2 memorise/learn **3** commemorate **4** keep
5 reminisce **6** jog **7** bring **8** recall/recollect
9 remind **10** recall/recollect

Ex D

2 reminder **3** nostalgia **4** memorial
5 memory **6** memento

Ex E

2A **3**F **4**B **5**C **6**E

Speaking Pages 78–79

Ex A

2 ✓
3 am going
4 had been learning/was learning/learned/learnt
5 ✓
6 is getting
7 will be working
8 will have been learning

Ex B

2 have been working ... am looking **3** to be getting **4** is studying ... am hoping/hope
5 am going/am going to go ... am planning/plan **6** were living **7** have been learning ... have been having **8** had been revising **9** is being built **10** had been living/lived/had lived

Ex C

2 German **3** history of Germany
4 linguistics

Ex D

2 like **3** trying **4** could/might

Ex E

2 ruled **3** protests **4** avoided

Ex F

2 failed **3** passed **4** take **5** set **6** takes/took
7 do **8** do

Writing Pages 80–82

Ex A

2 you to go to Russia, which cities would you like to visit?
3 the last Ice Age not ended when it did, our civilization might well not have developed.
4 the Romans not invaded Britain, Hadrian's Wall would never have been built.

Ex B

2 were children allowed

3 had the war ended
4 did they have/were they able
5 had he become
6 did a human walk
7 has there been
8 had/have they seen

Ex C
1 ever
2 much ... that
3 such
4 even
5 more

Ex D
2 of **3** which/that **4** while/when/made
5 making **6** which **7** Forgetting/Failing
8 during/in/after **9** where/when **10** whom

Ex E

Noun	Verb	Adjective
belief disbelief believer	believe disbelieve	believable unbelievable
doubt doubter	doubt	doubtful
evidence	-	evident self-evident

Adverb	Phrases
unbelievably	look/stare/etc. in disbelief contrary to popular belief
doubtless undoubtedly	doubting Thomas
evidently	-

Ex F
2 However/Nevertheless
3 While/Although
4 in my opinion/in my view
5 In the opinion of scientists/According to scientists
6 forward

Ex G

Bare infinitive	Past simple	Past participle
be	was/were	been
become	became	become
begin	began	begun
break	broke	broken
bring	brought	brought
build	built	built
buy	bought	bought
catch	caught	caught
choose	chose	chosen
come	came	come
cost	cost	cost
deal	dealt	dealt
do	did	done
drive	drove	driven
eat	ate	eaten
fight	fought	fought
find	found	found
forget	forgot	forgotten
get	got	got (gotten)
give	gave	given
go	went	gone/been
have	had	had
hear	heard	heard
hold	held	held
keep	kept	kept
know	knew	known
lead	led	led
leave	left	left
lose	lost	lost
make	made	made
put	put	put
read	read	read
say	said	said
see	saw	seen
sell	sold	sold
send	sent	sent
set	set	set
show	showed	shown
speak	spoke	spoken
spend	spent	spent
stand	stood	stood
steal	stole	stolen
take	took	taken
teach	taught	taught
tell	told	told
think	thought	thought
understand	understood	understood
win	won	won
write	wrote	written

Exam Practice Page 83

Ex A
2 pump **3** mines **4** surface **5** pipe **6** vacuum
7 pause **8** fuel **9** hammers **10** vehicles

Ex B
2 dominant **3** partial **4** conventional
5 sophisticated **6** circular **7** located
8 refined

Ex C
2 chill **3** condensed **4** suck **5** set
6 converting **7** up **8** adapt

Review Units 5–8 Pages 84–85

A
1B **2**A **3**D **4**B **5**D **6**D **7**C **8**A

B
1 evidence **2** fortunate **3** explanation
4 expertise **5** scientific **6** knowledgeable
7 harmful **8** significant **9** ability
10 argument

C
1 had I seen such a shocking sight!
2 Robert to speak to Alan (for me).
3 had gone to Moscow, we would have seen the festival.
4 he spoke did I realise he was French.
5 me to apply to university.
6 they to agree, we could sign the contract tomorrow.
7 watched the news, they would know what's / what was going on.
8 are having our new sofa delivered on Tuesday.

D
1 down **2** across **3** forward **4** on **5** up **6** up
7 over **8** up

E
1 to think **2** hadn't gone **3** have been coming **4** be getting **5** waiting **6** to be
7 did anyone ask **8** go

F
1 profound **2** conventional **3** partial
4 presentable **5** deliberate **6** persuasive
7 essential **8** precise

AUDIOSCRIPT

BSB CD, 1 (Listening Exercise E)

Young woman: I've always been interested in art, even from a very young age. We didn't have a gallery in my town, but I used to go to the library and borrow all the books on fine art. I loved the beautiful paintings and sculptures and could look at them for hours! As I got older, I began to travel around to see different kinds of art. I remember the first time I saw somebody doing performance art. It was a woman who covered herself in paint and then danced around as she read poetry! It was a bit strange, but I thought it was quite interesting.

Later on, I became interested in conceptual art. The best conceptual art presents a really strong idea that makes you see the world in a different way and maybe even shocks you. I saw one piece that was just a pile of rubbish. You wouldn't normally think it was art, but it actually said a lot about the way we damage the environment.

I think my favourite kind of art, though, is pop art. I love the kind of images you see in comics or in adverts, and some artists can do really clever things with them.

BSB CD, 2 (Speaking Exercise D)

Interviewer: Would you describe yourself as an artistic person?
Hélène: Well, I suppose I'm quite musical. I love music and I play several musical instruments. I've been playing the piano since I was about three years old and I also play the violin and the guitar. I got my first guitar when I was seven, so I've been playing for about thirteen years. I've actually also just started learning the trumpet – I have two lessons a week – but I'm not very good yet!
Interviewer: Do you have any hobbies other than music?
Hélène: Well, I'm not sure you can call it a hobby, but I love reading. I always take a book with me, wherever I go. I've almost finished reading Tolstoy's *War and Peace* – I've just got a few pages to go – so now I'm trying to decide what to read next. I want something different to *War and Peace*, so it'll probably be more modern – and shorter!

BSB CD, 3 (Speaking Exercise D)

Narrator: Speaker 1
Speaker 1: The government have just introduced a new law banning smoking in public places, and it's started a lot of discussion. Many people disagree with it. My personal opinion is that it's about time we did something like that.

Narrator: Speaker 2
Speaker 2: I read something about the new law against smoking in public places. It seems to me that it's just another way of controlling people, but I know that a large number of people think it's a good idea.

Narrator: Speaker 3
Speaker 3: I don't smoke, but some of my friends do. They've all been complaining about the law, although from my point of view, it should be a good way of encouraging people to give up.

Narrator: Speaker 4
Speaker 4: According to some people, this smoking ban is necessary to promote good health, by convincing people that it's a good idea to stop. I tend to think, though, that you should do it through education, rather than through the law.

Narrator: Speaker 5
Speaker 5: They were talking on the news about the new smoking law, and everyone seemed to welcome it. Well, as far as I'm concerned, it's an attack on personal freedom.

Narrator: Speaker 6
Speaker 6: There's a new law coming in, and it'll make it illegal to smoke in public places. In my opinion, it's a shame they've waited so long before introducing it, even if some people object to it.

BSB CD, 4 (Writing Exercise K)

Woman: It was unbelievable, really. I was coming home from work one day the usual way in the car, and as I drove through the town centre, I saw that there were quite a few police cars outside a bank. I wondered what was going on. Well, I drove on and just as I was pulling into my street, I noticed that there were more police cars there. It seemed strange, but I thought maybe they'd found evidence of a crime somewhere and they were investigating it. Well, when I got out of my car, the police came over and said they suspected me of being involved in a crime! I laughed and thought they were joking, but they arrested me for robbing the bank! They took me to the police station and charged me! I was in shock. They called my lawyer and put me in a cell. I was there for ten hours until they sorted it all out. Apparently, a car I used to own had been used in the robbery. Can you imagine what might have happened if I'd been found guilty of it? I wouldn't like to think.

BSB CD, 5 (Speaking Exercise D)

Interviewer: Do you think technology is going to change the way children learn at school?
Candidate: That's a good question. And yes, I do. But sometimes you hear people say 'Oh, in twenty years' time, <u>there aren't any</u> teachers. All the children are going to learn from computers and robots.' I don't really believe that. In fifty years' time, teachers will still be teaching, and children will still <u>have used</u> books too. Or at least I think so. Of course in, say, fifty years, things will have changed in the classroom enormously. Blackboards will have been replaced by smart boards, connected to the internet. Even in poorer countries, I imagine. And that'll be great when it <u>will happen</u>.

BSB CD, 6 (Writing Exercise I)

Female estate agent: So, this is the living room. It's a sizeable room for a semi-detached house, isn't it? I think it's surprisingly spacious. The whole place has just been cleaned thoroughly, and I think you'll agree it's completely spotless. If you look at the walls, you'll see there's a substantial number of electric sockets. More than enough for your needs, I'd have thought. The main feature of the room, of course, is this new full-height window here which overlooks the extensive garden. A significant amount of work has been done on the house and garden in the renovation, and the owners have spent a considerable amount of money on it. So, let's move into the kitchen…

BSB CD, 7 (Listening Exercise F)

Lecturer: Now of course when we're working with measurements we do have to be careful. Although many countries use the metric system today, other measurement systems are still in use and it's incredible how easy it is to make a mistake when converting

between them. The other system we're going to look at now is the imperial system.
So, in the metric system the standard unit of length or distance measurement is the metre. In the imperial system, we measure in inches, feet, yards and miles. An inch is 2.54 centimetres. There are twelve inches in a foot, and three feet in a yard. A yard is just a little bit shorter than a metre. It's actually 91.44 centimetres. In terms of miles, there are 1,760 yards in a mile. A mile, by the way, is considerably longer than a kilometre. It's just over 1,600 metres: 1,609.344 metres, to be precise.
In terms of weight, things get rather more complicated because the imperial gallon is different to the gallon used in the United States, so I think it's better [fade out] if we don't go into detail on that now…

BSB CD, 8 **(Speaking Exercise G)**

Narrator: one
Voice: I think I'd better go home now.
Narrator: two
Voice: I'm tired. I think I'm going to go to bed, if you don't mind.
Narrator: three
Voice: Right. I've got to go to work now. I'll see you this evening.
Narrator: four
Voice: Do you fancy going for a swim this afternoon?
Narrator: five
Voice: It's amazing how many people have never been abroad.
Narrator: six
Voice: We used to go camping a lot when I was a kid.
Narrator: seven
Voice: Do you want to go sightseeing, or would you rather just sit in a café somewhere?
Narrator: eight
Voice: We went on a really interesting tour of the castle.
Narrator: nine
Voice: How do you get to work? Do you go by train or bus?
Narrator: ten
Voice: You can't drive down to the beach. You have to go on foot.

BSB CD, 9 **(Listening Exercise D)**

Young woman: I got a new computer a week ago. I got it home and couldn't wait to use it because it was much better than my old computer. I took it out of the box and plugged everything in. Then I switched it on. It worked fine for a couple of hours, and then it just broke down while I was surfing the internet. It completely died and I had no idea what was wrong with it. I tried everything to find out what the problem was, but it just wouldn't work. Eventually, I came up with the idea of using my old computer to connect to the internet to see if I could find some advice. I searched and searched and finally I found a website with comments from people who had had the same problem with that model of computer. It said that there was a problem with the processor and that I had to take it to a computer shop so they could carry out repairs. It was so annoying! I finally got it back today. Let's hope it doesn't break down again!

BSB CD, 10 **(Writing Exercise I)**

Narrator: Speaker 1
Speaker 1: This range of mountains was formed when two large plates of the Earth's crust collided with each other, forcing a large amount of material up.
Narrator: Speaker 2
Speaker 2: It's clear from these bits of pottery that the ancient Romans had very well-established trade routes with a number of different peoples.
Narrator: Speaker 3
Speaker 3: Of course, there are almost no tribes that have literally had no contact with the outside world, but there are some where that has been kept to a minimum.
Narrator: Speaker 4
Speaker 1: The heart pumps the blood into the aorta, and from there it travels to tissues, bringing oxygen and taking away the waste products.
Narrator: Speaker 5
Speaker 5: We may feel as if we are in control of our thoughts, but it seems that this may be an illusion and there is a lot going on that we are not aware of.
Narrator: Speaker 6
Speaker 6: These clouds form at an altitude of 10,000 feet, where a region of warm air is forced upwards by a region of colder air.

BSB CD, 11 **(Listening Exercise B)**

Narrator: Speaker 1
Speaker 1: My role largely happens before anyone else is involved. I might go to them with an idea, or they might come to me. Whichever way round it is, I usually have a few months to come up with an initial version, which is then analysed and reworked. I'm rarely involved once they start shooting, but they might occasionally call me to clarify something.
Narrator: Speaker 2
Speaker 2: I'm focused on making sure we make the right programmes for the right audience. I'm responsible for all drama programmes, so there's a lot to think about. Once we've got a show in production, I tend not to get too involved and just leave the people I've chosen to get on with it. Of course, at the end of the day, I need to approve everything.
Narrator: Speaker 3
Speaker 3: I'm the one who decides exactly what we're going to shoot on the day. It involves choosing the right camera angles, as well as working with the actors to make sure they're comfortable with what they're doing. It's the decisions I make that really bring the script to life.
Narrator: Speaker 4
Speaker 4: There's a lot of waiting between shots while everyone gets things ready, followed by a few minutes of intense concentration. When I'm performing, I try to forget that all the equipment is there and focus on what I'm trying to communicate. I hate making mistakes with lines because I know that it means everyone has to start again.
Narrator: Speaker 5
Speaker 5: A large part of my job is making sure that we don't go over budget. I have to approve all spending. I'm also responsible for making sure that we keep to the schedule. Even just a few days over can cost the company a lot of money.

BSB CD, 12 (Writing Exercise F)

Lecturer: I'd like now to look at the ways in which regulation of the media developed in the United States of America from the '40s onwards. The first changes were brought about as a result of a rule which placed a limit on the ownership of radio and TV stations. The rule prevented anybody from owning stations which could be received by more than 35% of the people living in the country. Consequently, the power of media companies was restricted. Five years later, in 1946, more regulations were introduced, which this time prevented large media companies from buying others of a similar size.
This increasing regulation of the media continued over the next three decades. In 1970, the power of broadcasters was weakened further, due to a rule which prevented anyone from owning a radio station and a television station broadcasting to the same audience. Other similar rules followed later in the '70s.
In the late '70s and early '80s, some people began to feel that the extent of the regulation of the media was unreasonable and gradually the rules were relaxed. In '85 the rule that placed a limit on the total number of advertisements a station could broadcast per hour was removed. Two years later, one of the biggest changes happened when they got rid of the Fairness Doctrine. That rule had required stations to show both sides of an argument, and once it had gone, stations were free to present stories how they liked. Almost a decade after that, in 1996, the rule limiting ownership of radio stations was lifted, which meant that large companies were free to buy as many as they could afford.
Now, let's look at some of the changes that have taken place since 1996.

BSB CD, 13 (Reading Exercise D)

Male lecturer: So now let's come on to languages where you can't simply take the name of the country and change the ending. Don't make the mistake – as many people do – of saying that in America they speak American. They don't. They speak English, though it can be described as a form of English called American English. Likewise in Canada, there's no such thing as Canadian in terms of language. Once again, it's English, though of course Canada has two official languages, the other being French.
Similarly, there's no such language as Indian. In India, more than 24 languages are spoken widely. English is often used for official purposes, and other recognised languages include Hindi, Bengali, Gujarati, Punjabi and Urdu.
Urdu is also the national language of Pakistan, though English is recognised as the official language, and is the language used in the constitution and often for business. There are a number of regional languages in use in Pakistan too. Six main ones, including Punjabi.
And what's the official language of the Netherlands, or Holland? It's Dutch. Forms or varieties of Dutch are also spoken throughout Belgium. These are often also known as Flemish.

BSB CD, 14 (Listening Exercise D)

Female lecturer: Gestures around the world vary depending on culture. In Britain, a number of gestures are used regularly. British people often nod their head to signify confirmation or approval. Basically, this gesture means 'yes'. When people shake their head, they are expressing the opposite: negation or disapproval. Basically, then, this gesture means 'no'. When people in Britain tut – that is, they make a small audible click with the tongue – that is also a sign of disapproval.
Another sign of disapproval, often used by parents to small children, is to wag your finger. This involves a small sideways movement of the index finger several times. To wave is to move the whole hand with the same movement several times. This is used for greetings and saying goodbye.
To wink at someone – that is, to quickly close and then open one eye – usually indicates that the person doing it recognises a shared secret or shared information between them and the person they are doing it to. It's often considered a humorous, naughty or cheeky gesture, and is usually only used informally.
If you roll your eyes, you rotate both eyes upwards for a short time. This can be used to express a number of negative emotions including boredom, disbelief annoyance and impatience.

BSB CD, 15 (Listening Exercise E)

Narrator: Speaker 1
Male: Hi Alan. Don't forget the time of the meeting this afternoon's been changed and it's starting at three o'clock now. Okay?

Narrator: Speaker 2
Female: Well of course when I was a child there was much less crime and violence than there is now. I suppose we didn't have so much disposable income, but we were definitely happier. Life was so much better back then, you know.

Narrator: Speaker 3
Male: Actually Ellen gave me this book the last time I ever saw her, so I have to say it's got a very special place in my heart.

Narrator: Speaker 4
Female: It's a funny thing, isn't it? I mean, ask me what I did on my birthday fifteen years ago and I can tell you. Ask me where I've just put the car keys, and I haven't the faintest idea!

Narrator: Speaker 5
Male: This is the statue, with the names of all the people who died in the accident on this plaque here. We have a small service once a year to remember them. It's very touching, even though it all happened a long time ago.

Narrator: Speaker 6
Female: I bet you can guess where we were when Brian got this. Casablanca! Well, I know it's a bit predictable, but if you don't come back with one of these red hats after you've been to Morocco, no-one's going to believe you actually went there, are they?

BSB CD, 16 (Speaking Exercise C)

Young woman: Yes, I do enjoy learning languages. I suppose it's about seven years now since I started learning English. I have three lessons a week, plus all the homework, so it's quite hard but I still enjoy it. In fact, I enjoy learning languages so much that I've recently started having German lessons. The grammar is quite difficult, but I'm also learning a lot about the history of Germany, which is very interesting. I think an understanding of the history and culture of a place really helps you learn the language. My aim is to go to university somewhere like the United States and do linguistics, so the more I know about different languages, the better.